D0481825

'93

California Currents

California Currents

An Exploration of the Ocean's Pleasures, Mysteries, and Dilemmas

Marie De Santis

Illustrations by Patricia Walker
Foreword by Michael Herz

★
PRESIDIO

Library of Congress Cataloging in Publication Data

De Santis, Marie, 1945–
    California currents.

    Includes index.
    1. Oceanography — Pacific Coast (Calif.)
2. Environmental protection — Pacific Coast (Calif.)
3. Pacific Coast (Calif.) 4. Marine resources —
Pacific Coast (Calif.) 5. Ocean. I. Title.
GC856.D47   1985   508.3164'32   84-14115
ISBN 0-89141-191-7

Printed in the United States of America

To my Mom and Dad, and Martin, Danny, and Eileen

Contents

Foreword

Although I had read and enjoyed Marie De Santis's exciting first book, *Neptune's Apprentice*, I was not prepared for her present effort. As she began work on this project, she explained that she was going to do a book on the California coast, marine resource management, and the institutions involved in research on the ocean—hardly the stuff that keeps you on the edge of your seat.

But as anyone who has read Marie's writing should know, she has a unique way of weaving together folklore, philosophy, science, and fishing into a fabric that is both great fun and highly educational at the same time. One of the many problems faced by those of us who spend our lives trying to study, protect, and manage oceans and coastlines is that there are not enough people around who are aware of the various threats to the marine environment or who care to try to make things better. We—the professionals in this business—are at fault for not educating the public about these important issues. Marie De Santis educates—with humor, wisdom, and compassion—in a way we never have been able to.

I first heard about Marie as "the only woman commercial fisherman in the Bay Area." She seems to thrive on such contradictions, from being a flatlander graduate student in chemistry at the University of Chicago to fishing the California coast to working with abused and abandoned children. While the author obviously has great love and respect for the sea and creatures that live there, she is no whale hugger. She sees the ocean, fish, and sea mammals as part of an important reality—"part of the roundness of things." But she is concerned about the degree to which people romanticize whales and dolphins, creating a "bambiology" cult that denies the harsh reality of a nature in which species interact, some living on others.

Marie De Santis also introduces us to what might be called the zen of fishing. She counsels us to find a good fishing spot and then to follow one strict, unbreakable rule—"Don't ever allow a conclusion to become fully jelled in your mind." While she really seems to be saying that all generalizations are bad, she is also telling us never to be satisfied with a single conclusion about anything.

California Currents contrasts the reality of the sea with the folklore of fishing tradition; it intersperses marine policy and law of the sea deliberations with fish recipes. What is most striking about reading this book is that one can learn how the ocean works —how to farm it, manage it, mine it, measure its pollutants, and how to catch and culture its inhabitants. In short, it is a truly unique book that will educate, entertain, and illuminate anyone who reads it, regardless of his or her background.

Perhaps the reason this book is so appealing is that it presents a philosophy, as well as showing us what happens in the sea. My enthusiasm about it stems largely from the fact that I am not used to being entertained while at the same time being given refreshingly new perspectives about marine science and policy. At this time in the history of our planet (and it should be recalled that almost three quarters of "earth" is covered with water), we are facing tremendous pressures on our oceans, for food, minerals, and oil. And our coastal areas, the most productive areas of the ocean, are under the heaviest fishing pressures they have ever seen. This is why it is important to have a book such as this, which can give so many people a perspective from which to consider these important resources. Marie De Santis is to be congratulated for having found her medium. She has the unique ability to bring the ocean, its inhabitants, and philosophy (both it and hers) together into a truly important book.

Michael Herz
Senior Vice President,
Oceanic Society

Acknowledgments

My gratitude to:

My friend Patty Walker whose fine artwork enhances the images of the sea throughout the book.

My editor at Presidio Press, Joan Griffin, for her sensitive copiloting of my writing projects.

Zeke Grader of the Pacific Coast Federation of Fishermen, Mike Herz of the Oceanic Society, and John McCosker of Steinhart Aquarium, for some great leads.

The over two hundred sailors, scientists, fishermen, fish farmers, ocean miners, dolphin trainers, Fish and Game officials, lawyers, policymakers, environmentalists, and engineers who, when I asked to talk with them for a book about the ocean, responded unanimously with "How much time do you need?"

Introduction

Throughout the full spectrum of California's diverse population, the sound of the surf and the lure of the distant horizon exert a singular pull. There isn't a soul who can stand at the shore, look out over the vast watery expanse, and not be given to wonder. Instinctively, you know there's a whole lot more going on out there than meets the eye: a different set of rules, an alien pulse of life, quite apart from even the most extreme forms that have been generated by land. And that mystery has a grip of intense power and infinite beauty that inevitably pulls you in.

After eight years of making my living at sea, however, I returned to the beach feeling that I had had enough intensity and infinity for a lifetime. But leisure hours and free time soon found me wandering again at the water's edge. It was obvious that the sea's intrigue is not so easily extinguished. Still, my desire to continue exploring the ocean's mysteries at the whims of my curiosity seemed as remote a fantasy as the desire to be a child again. Until I approached Presidio Press with the idea of writing it down. "Sounds like a great idea," they said.

In the months that followed I meandered through aquariums, trekked through estuaries, clambered aboard ships, hung out with sailors in the Union Halls, submerged myself in libraries, observed in laboratories, and in the process asked everyone I met along the way every question I had about the ocean.

The only constraint we placed on the project was to confine the territory to the California ocean. This, because even though an individual may not know the California Current from the tropical trades, we automatically have an intuitive relationship to the environment in which we live, if only through the air we breathe. This constraint, however, proved no more a restriction than limiting questions of the universe to the Milky Way galaxy. California's ocean exemplifies the mysteries of the sea in their fullest intensity. It's surprising how few people are aware of the massive upwellings, the powerful currents, the broad fertile shelf that make our own backyard one of the richest, most dynamic stretches of ocean in the world.

Add to this the full-blooded mixture of Californians themselves—the go-getters, money-makers, sun-worshipers, saviors, sinners, and survivors—all of us poised here at the edge of the sea with "Go West!" still coursing through our veins, and you can be sure that the human activities at sea are as dynamic as the waters themselves. In the past two decades, the whole world ocean has been transformed from the unfathomable space between the continents to a frontier territory on the center stage of world events, a condensation of the same history that took thousands of years on land. Nowhere have these events resonated more profoundly than along our western coast.

The forty-five essays that follow proceed from topics of oceanography to sea life to ocean issues, but only in the loosest sense, as I have made no attempt to unweave the natural connections between them. It will also be evident from a random thumb through the book that it is not meant to be comprehensive. Instead I have chosen to turn the kaleidoscope on impulse, to leave juxtapositions unharmonized and let currents of thought mix, collide, and submerge as they do in the sea. If after using this book, you have more questions than answers, then its purpose is served—to heighten your sense of wonder.

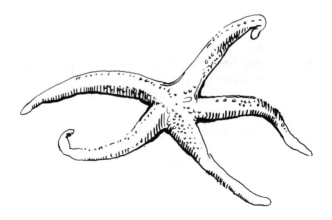

Chapter 1

Point Conception

Though it seems rather haphazardly situated two thirds of the way down the California coast, Point Conception is a good beginning, and not just because of its name. It marks a sharp boundary in the character of our ocean. Above this point are the cold, treacherous, murky green waters of the northeast Pacific, which have more in common with the waters of Alaska than they do with the warm and soothing blue seas just to the south of the point. California, in fact, has two very distinct oceans.

From the land, Point Conception isn't much different from our other grassy headlands—a great sweep of treeless rangeland that juts out and up into the sky, then plummets suddenly down a rocky cliff to the sea. Stand at its edge and a whole continent of worries dissolves behind you as boundlessness unfurls in front. It's a vantage point that can be had all along the coast; it's the view, in fact, that populated the state. From the land, Point Conception reveals nothing of its rougish reputation among the people of the sea.

Ralph Hazard started fishing out of Santa Barbara with his dad when he was eleven years old. His stomping grounds are the waters from San Diego up to Monterey Bay, but most of his years have been spent around Point Conception, and he knows the area well. "You leave Santa Barbara," he says, "and maybe you'll have a little light breeze coming from the south. Then you get up around Gaviota and it's like somebody drew a line across the sea, the water turns all white. And if you're in tight to the kelp, like any reasonable person should be with a small boat, you'll be getting some good winds coming down off the shore. Then you start feeling a heavy westerly swell, and when you get up to the point it's like hitting a wall; everything's in your face. The strong northwesterly wind, a steep westerly sea and chop that's sharp and nasty, and if you get the tide running against it—which happens often—all hell breaks loose. Those rollers start to break, and it makes a hell of a mess.

"A couple of days ago, one of the oil boats, one about a hundred and fifty feet long, was going up on the outside, and one of those waves went all the way up on his deck and washed a man overboard. A lot of times there's only one way to deal with that place. You head back to the shore and go into Government Cove just below the point and anchor for the duration. You'll do a little rolling around in there, no doubt about that, but at least you'll be around to give it another shot. But don't get the impression it's just some mean weather you'll find at the point. There's a lot more going on up there than meets the eye. I've seen big schools of sea bass go right up to Point Conception and then turn around and go back and hide behind the point till things are more to their liking. It's not the waves that are stopping them; it's big changes in the current and the water itself. You go up around Point Conception, and it's another world."

John McGowan is an oceanographer at Scripps who has spent

much of his life studying the California Current. He is working as a member of the CalCOFI Team (California Cooperative Oceanic Fisheries Investigations), a unique, world-renowned research group that literally erupted out of one of the most bitter arguments ever to occur on the coast. When the sardine disappeared in 1946, fingers were pointed every which way, and a few fists, too. The fish industry, fed up with taking the blame, taxed itself a dollar a ton for the purpose of funding a diverse group of researchers to prove once and for all that overfishing was not the cause. The group, people from the state Department of Fish and Game, Scripps Institute, the federal Fisheries Service, the California Academy, and the industry itself, was brought together kicking and screaming, but they were forced to cooperate by the large amounts of money involved and the severity of the question at hand. "But," says John, "the remarkable thing is that the group has continued. And in those same thirty years it has produced the only long-term study of the physics and biology of an oceanic system. The California Current is the best-understood marine ecosystem in the world.

"It's a broad, slow, meandering current that originates in Alaska. We know this because its salinity is relatively low compared to the central Pacific Ocean of the same latitude. Its outer boundary is about four hundred miles offshore in the San Francisco area and about six hundred miles offshore at San Diego. Its meanderings produce large eddies sometimes a hundred and fifty to two hundred miles in diameter. The eddies lounge around for a while and then disappear. The current goes through seasonal changes, too. It speeds up in the spring, gets most intense in July, and around August it starts to weaken. By early winter it's at its weakest, so weak that it allows water from the central gyre (the giant circular surface current) to move in closer to the shore. There is also a deep undercurrent in California that goes up the coast on the bottom over the continental shelf. And there is the Davidson Current that comes up from Baja and moves very inshore; whether or not it gets above Conception, we don't know."

"What's going on at Point Conception?" I asked, certain that, of all people, he would know.

"Well," he answered, "the waters above the point are uniformly colder and fresher than the waters to the south. It's also much windier and rougher to the north. Point Conception is, in addition, a marked biological boundary, both on the shore and in the open ocean. Below the point you see animals like the barracuda, the lobster, and the mackerels, and above you see the salmonids. North of Point Conception, the water also has a much higher plankton count and much more life of all kinds."

"But why is it that Point Conception is the dividing line?"

"Oh," he said, *"that's* what you want to know. Oh boy, I wish I knew, but it sure as hell is. One thing I do know is that there is a big wobble in the California Current right at Point Conception, and whether that has something to do with it or not, I just don't know. Thirty years is a long time relative to other ocean studies, but compared to comparable systems on the land, we haven't even begun."

This is probably the most unanimous sentiment I encountered among the two hundred people I interviewed in the course of writing this book: we haven't even begun to study the sea. Despite the fact that the ocean lies right in the backyard of one of the busiest and hustlingest peoples on earth, its mysteries have barely been named. This question about Point Conception was one of half a dozen questions that I tended to ask of everyone along the way. Only once did I get an answer to this one that was immediate, assured, and to the point. Philip Vella has fished the length of the California coast for sixty-eight years, but unlike Ralph Hazard, he has fished most of that time in northern waters. "Point Conception?" he said without a moment's hesitation. "God walks on the water below that point, and all the water above it He left to the devil."

Chapter 2

At Sea

How many miles from your home to the shore? Add only thirty or forty to that and it would put you on the high sea—the water beyond the horizon where land no longer exists, not even for your anchor. It's a distance you wouldn't think twice about traveling to the east or south or north, but due west is a different story. Yet the people who spend months and months at a time out there say the salt gets in your blood and you have to go back again. And it must be true.

Just watch the behavior of fishermen or sailors who have been on the beach too long. As they restlessly roam the wharves, unable to venture inland farther than the salt air smell, it's obvious their spirits have already embarked. For some people, life on the open sea becomes an intractable need, as if some permanent split has formed in their being and can never be fused again, or denied. The poet John Masefield named the lure, probably as closely as it can be named: "I must down to the seas again, to the lonely sea and the sky." It's so eloquently simple beyond the horizon—there is only the sea and the sky; that's all you have to know.

In the late summer and early fall off the coast of California, the northwest winds die down, and so does the wind-driven California Current. Warm water from the central Pacific Gyre moves in to our coast, and with it come the albacore on their annual swing through the northeast Pacific. About three thousand California fishermen give chase, roaming up to Vancouver Island, down to Mexico, out three or four hundred miles, around and about and back again. They make trips lasting up to thirty days. There are even some children who grow up out there: like Cindy who has spent over half of her life at sea since she was three years old. She started out cleaning hooks, and by the age of six she had a full-time position in the stern pulling fish. And whenever the fish weren't biting, she used to work on her correspondence classes on a rolling galley table.

The San Diego and San Pedro tunamen leave on trips to the open sea that average ninety days at a stretch. The whole tropical Pacific is their range, from Guam to New Zealand, from Samoa to Central America. Merchant sailors make trips that last for months and months and months, with only the most fleeting stops in port. They come home for a while, and then they go back and do it again.

Who among the most firmly entrenched on land hasn't at one time or another stood on the shore and dreamed of doing the same? In reality, putting your bow on the horizon is even more heavenly than you could ever imagine. Watching a whole continent shrink in your wake feels like slipping a force as powerful as gravity. The freedom from land is euphoric. No matter the course, your boat is forever the center of a perfect circle wrapped only in horizons, with the days and nights flipping like pages through the sky. Life at sea is divested of a thousand burdensome garments that have muted the forces beneath their cloak. The weave of the great rhythms and cycles is exposed, and there you are confronted with the most unfathomable imaginings of dimension and depth that are, at once, the daily chores of your life.

The fishermen call it being on the outside. Someone who's on the beach is on the inside. And back and forth they go throughout their lives, being on the inside and then being on the outside, unable to quench the yearning for either side.

The land, too, has a pull, as strong as the sea's; don't think it doesn't. After a time at sea, simple thoughts of the land start drifting through your mind—walking on the stillness of the dock, a cup of coffee at a noisy restaurant, the face of a special person who's been waiting on the inside. You get on the radio and announce to the rest of the fleet, "I've reached," and everybody knows you're on the long tack, headed for the barn. The infinite has become too inescapable; the vision has stretched too far. It's time to touch the land.

No reunion is sweeter than tying the lines to the dock. For the first few days your walking feels like a strut. Your size is inflated in a world built snugly around your needs. You can go about your business and cavort with your friends without considering the void. But it isn't long before you notice that nothing moves and nothing holds your gaze, and once again, the open sea becomes a restless, restless need.

Chapter 3

Eastern Boundary Regions

A rather dull sounding topic, "eastern boundary regions," but stick with it and by the end of these pages henceforth this phrase will well up in your mind a new image of our most fertile state. California is one of four areas in the world that are described as eastern boundary regions; the west coast of South Africa, the Canary Island region, and the Peru-Chile coast share the distinction. The name refers to the narrow band of waters that hug the coasts of these regions. Together they occupy less than one thousandth of the world ocean surface and produce over one third of the world's fish. Of all the great natural wonders in California, the upwelling phenomena characteristic of these regions are the most spectacular of all. It is also mostly unheard of by the people who live by its edge and experience its effects every day. It requires only a little oceanography to explain.

Most of the world's ocean is desert. It's a great misconception to look at the abundance of fish near the shore and assume that it goes on like that forever. Life requires light, oxygen, and basic nutrition; nitrates and phosphates are primary. Light doesn't penetrate the ocean much beyond sixty feet, but even in the illuminated surface regions, the ocean is still mostly desert. The limiting factor is the lack of nutrients. The precious phosphate and nitrate fertilizers lie uselessly on the seafloor in the darkness of the deep.

When wind traverses the sea, it generates a movement of surface water that veers off on a course that is to the right of the direction of the wind. Here's why. Picture a slowly turning record on a turntable. Now picture putting your finger on the outer edge of the record and moving it in a straight line toward the center. And you see that though your finger went straight, the line it traced on the record veers to one side—because the record is turning, like the earth! So, too, the movement of water is rerouted by a force called the Coriolis force, resulting from the spin of the earth.

The temperate zone of the northern hemisphere is characterized by prevailing northwest winds, and in the mirror-image conditions in the southern hemisphere, the temperate zone is characterized by prevailing southwest winds. As these winds cross the open ocean, the surface waters that are moved to the side are merely replaced by the surface waters behind them. But when the severe northwest winds of our spring and summer whip down parallel to our coast and the great volumes of surface water are directed out to sea, there is only land behind. But the water does not go unreplaced. The new water comes from the deep, sucked to the surface in great plumes and fountains that boil and churn along the coast—cold, deep ocean water, full of nitrates and phosphates, silicates, and other nutrients. And when this water hits the light, it literally ignites in explosive blooms of plankton, for miles and miles and miles a richness of life and fertility unlike any other ocean area of the world, except for the other eastern boundary regions.

On the west coast of the United States, this upwelling is the strongest, by far, between Point Conception and Cape Mendocino. Here is one of the great fishing areas of the world—the biggest fish, the most fish, with the greatest density and diversity of life. The Russians, the Poles, the Japanese, the Koreans don't send their 300-foot fishing ships to our coast because fuel is cheap.

How many times have you listened to comments from tourists who say that our water is dirty? Shame no more! Tell them the water is murky, not dirty; the light can't penetrate the water, the plankton is so dense. And when you go to the tropics and look through the crystal-clear waters straight down to the bottom thirty or forty feet below, think about why it's so clear. There's nothing in it. Despite the narrow fringe reefs of beautiful but tiny fish, the waters of the north are many times more productive than the waters of the tropics, and in the upwelling regions, the factor is many times more. If you want sun, by all means go to the tropics, but if you're looking for good fishing, don't waste your money. It's right here in our own front yard.

In addition to the upwelling and fertility, we have quite a bit more in common with our far-flung regional cousins than you might expect. One, of course, is the icy cold water—and the excruciating, numbing pain that comes with putting your foot in it. Another is the fog. The warm, moisture-laden air coming in from offshore hits the cold, upwelled waters on the coast, and it's instant fog. Whether it's in the Atacama Desert, or the western Sahara, or the Namib Desert of South Africa, or the streets of San Francisco, it's the same "white, billowing plumes" or "gray and miserable mists," depending only on your mood. The climates, temperatures, and seasonal changes are also comparable for all four regions. But what seems even more amazing to me is that the species of fish, despite the fact that the regions are separated by thousands of miles, are nearly identical. And so are their relationships in the food chain. These regions are characterized by astounding volumes of the small pelagic fishes—sardines, anchovies, mackerels, and hake. The anchoveta fishery in Peru, by itself, made that country the top fish producer in the world for a very long time—until the fishery collapsed.

And this is proving to be another shared characteristic of the eastern boundary regions: the fisheries are subject to sudden, almost instantaneous collapse. The California sardine went first, then the North African sardine, then the Peruvian anchoveta, then the Cape Town sardine. And in each case, one fish was replaced by the other — California now has the anchovy, and the sardine turned up in Peru (but in much smaller numbers than the original stock, so far). Why this is so is the subject of more arguments, symposiums, and international meetings than ten books could summarize. The alternative answers, however, are quite simple: it's either the natural cyclical oceanic swings that are also characteristic of these regions, or it's overfishing. The reason for the friction is obvious; the reason for the inability to come up with the answer is that so little is known. It's only in the last few decades that anyone has even bothered to look at these eastern boundary regions that cover one thousandth of the ocean's surface and produce over one third of the world's fish.

Chapter 4

The Monterey Canyon

Unlike the rugged, precipitous cliffs of most of California's coast, at Monterey the land comes easily to the sea, and long, white-sand beaches lie on the verge. Nothing at all to indicate that a few yards beyond lies the upper ledge of a canyon that is deeper and steeper than the Grand Canyon in Arizona. If you leave on a boat from Moss Landing (between Monterey and Santa Cruz), the bottom falls away in spectacular vertical drops the moment you leave the jetty. From there, the axis of the canyon runs to the southwest and cuts in front of Cypress Point, where less than three miles off the beach the water is over a half mile deep, and a few more miles off-shore it drops down to 8,400 feet, the deep ocean abyss. The steepest vertical drops, however, occur right in Monterey Bay. According to those who have visualized the system in three dimensions, if all the water were drained out of the bay, those lying on the beach could look out over their toes and gaze across the grandest canyon of all. And the fact that the Monterey Canyon is submerged only adds to the grandeur of the events that occur within its rim.

Moss Landing Marine Labs is located only a few sandy yards south of the jetty. Like most other marine labs in the state, Moss Landing is the marine research and education facility for a consortium of colleges and universities in the area. Also like the others in the state, most of their research is focused on other parts of the world. Here at Moss Landing their primary interest is in looking at the vertical transport and exchange of trace elements through the sea; most of this work is being done on-site in Mexico and Peru. The director of the lab, John Martin, expressed a sentiment that I would hear again and again as I visited different labs. "What happens here along the coast," he said, "is pretty insignificant unless you're a fisherman." The funding for this research project is coming from a consortium of ocean mining firms, and the reason the study is so important, he says, is that "every jet plane has two hundred pounds of cobalt in its construction."

There are a couple of people here, however, who feel that the water outside their window is more than just a view—marine biologist Greg Cailliet, for one. He has the biggest collection of deep ocean sharks in the world, all of them caught within a half mile of the lab in the shallow flats alongside the head of the canyon. Monterey Bay is full of deep ocean species that get funneled up the canyon and spilled out over its lip.

John Broenkow is another. He's a physical oceanographer who's been looking at the tumultuous current systems in the canyon. He has applied to the National Science Foundation for a grant to study the relationship between these currents and the concentration of deep ocean species at the head of the canyon. From previous measurements, it is already known that the water coming out of the canyon has a very high salinity, is much colder than the surrounding water in the bay, and is loaded with phosphates and nitrates—all the earmarks of very deep ocean water. This and other nearshore canyons along the coast (Cape Mendocino is fronted by a number of canyons of nearly the same size as Monterey Canyon) may be vital taps to a kind of water that not even normal upwelling brings to the surface.

They also know that there is a net flow of water *out* of the canyon into the bay. One possibility is that this is due to tidal pumping. The tide waves move faster through the deep canyon than across the shallower bottom of the rest of the bay, so when the tide comes up out of the canyon it is pushed to the north by the bay's own current system, and when the tide goes back out through the canyon it takes a different body of water. Another possibility is that the offshore movement of wind-driven water supplies the pull for the net upward flow. Neither explanation, however, fully accounts for what is found when current meters are placed on the bottom of the canyon. The tremendous fluctuations of current direction don't seem to correlate with either the wind or the tide.

Another thing that has been discovered about the canyon is that it is geologically a very active place. While diving around its edge in the course of other studies, they have observed large-scale collapses, or slumps, around the sides and on the flats. Even on shore they see the effects. Not long ago, Moss Landing Marine Labs lost part of its fence to a slump. The canyon is full of geological faults. "I get nervous anytime there is an earthquake anywhere in the area," says John. "If they had known what was going on down there, they would never have built this lab where it is. Any day we could all get slumped right out of a job."

Chapter 5

Tijuana Slough

In 1972, Congress passed the Marine Protection, Research, and Sanctuaries Act, which authorized the secretary of commerce to designate ocean areas with special value as marine sanctuaries. In 1977, National Oceanic and Atmospheric Administration (NOAA), the lead agency for this program, began soliciting suggestions from regional groups on the most deserving locations. By 1984, California had four marine sanctuaries, all in early stages of development, still feeling out their sense of direction, and all of them open to projects and the participation of the general public.

The Point Reyes–Farallons site was selected primarily because it is the main breeding ground for many of the state's seabirds and encompasses important breeding and feeding areas for nearly all species of the California Current. The Channel Islands Sanctuary was selected because of its similar importance for the wildlife of our southern waters. Elkhorn Slough (located in Moss Landing) and the Tijuana Slough were chosen because both are estuaries. Estuaries are the nurseries of the sea; there are very few of them on the west coast, and they are the marine environment most susceptible to destruction by human activity.

Of all these locations, Tijuana Slough, by almost any measure, is certainly the most intriguing. In fact, I would guess it is the most bizarre place on earth ever to be labeled a sanctuary. Tijuana Slough is considered the most pristine estuary south of San Francisco Bay and is one of the few remaining natural estuaries in the entire United States. But stand anywhere in the twenty-five hundred acres of marsh, at any time of the day or night, and you'll see half a dozen helicopters hovering overhead with the brazenness of well-entrenched native birds: Navy helicopters, Coast Guard helicopters, Army, and Border Patrol—the entire species represented in its full spectrum of colors.

Tijuana Slough is also the Mexican border. The dusty Mexican town of Tijuana sits on its ridge, and the bullring fills the air with the roar of the crowds. But it's during the night that Mexico truly inhabits the marsh. For years, the setting sun has transformed these primeval bogs into a golden highway of promise. Every night, a hundred Mexicans trudge through the grass and the mud, stomping out a life of despair, despite the sensors placed throughout the marsh, despite the helicopters and the trucks that stand waiting on the other side. In the morning, as many are loaded into trucks and returned, save for the one who made it, ensuring the return of the next night's run. And perhaps it all balances out, as it is the border that saved the marsh.

Pollution, oil spills, and bombs are the things you might think are destroying the earth. But highways and railroads, the arteries of our way of life, have suffocated more acres than the others combined. Build a railroad or highway across an estuary, and the hundreds of rivulets that nurture it are severed. Our way of life doesn't cross the border, however, and the roadway across the slough was never built. The mullet and halibut still come into the protected, quiet waters to spawn, trusting their millions of larvae to the rich plankton soup that grows from the decay of the marsh. And the migrating birds from Alaska, Canada, and the northern United States still come down here for the winter to eat. And the Tijuana River that feeds the marsh? It's got problems, to be sure. Half the water of the river comes from the mountains behind the slough, and the other half is untreated sewage from the town of Tijuana, so much sewage that the ocean frontage is currently quarantined by the city of San Diego and the slough itself has been given accolades as the nation's only turd sanctuary. But still, the river is alive! It meanders, spreads, seeps, eddies, and filters its way through the estuary in a thousand capillaries that bring life to the cells of the marsh.

Look at Mission Bay, thirty miles to the north in the heart of San Diego. Lysol clean. Not a view anywhere to offend the eye: acres of manicured golf courses, and shorelines of carefully placed rocks; miles and miles of walking paths fit for your Sunday shoes; and the palms and willows landscaped like the plaza at city hall. Whales used to come into Mission Bay! And pickleweed grew in the mud on its shores. The estuary died a sanitary death, incapable even of decaying itself back to life.

Paul Jorgensen's job is to oversee the management of Tijuana Slough Sanctuary. He started in 1983, and after a few months it was clear to him why not too many others had applied for the job. Paul is a zoologist who has worked for the U.S. Fish and Wildlife Service and the Department of Fish and Game; he's assessed resources for independent contracting companies and for a few years was responsible for overseeing endangered species management on naval property. Interestingly, Paul did his thesis right here in the slough, trudging through the byways with his binoculars, observing quietly for hours as one of the slough's most established residents went about its daily routine. Paul had chosen the light-footed clapper rail for his study, in part because it is an endangered species and he was thus likely to be funded to study it, but also because this unassuming little hen is the best indicator we have of the health of a marsh. The clapper rail lives its entire life in the marsh and makes use of all the layers of the system. Day or night for six days a week, Paul watched contentedly as the clapper rail showed him how it is done.

Those days are over for Paul. There are over fifty agencies with jurisdiction in the Tijuana Slough, and many of these jurisdictions overlap. "My job," says Paul, trying bravely to be nonchalant, "is to manage this area as a unit without usurping any power from the agencies that are already here. So you can see why a lot of people who were qualified didn't even want to be considered for the job." The same problem exists at all the other sanctuaries along the coast, but in addition, Paul has to negotiate internationally. "Something has to be done about the sewage problem because it's getting worse, but Mexico is a very poor country and the solution isn't going to happen overnight." It was nature that dealt him the worst blow of all: "The storms from all the El Niño weather [warm ocean current] we've been having pushed so much sand across the entrance to the slough that the tidal flushing has been reduced by 75 percent." Ironically, the first action of the sanctuary team was to intervene in nature, by dredging the entrance to reopen it to tidal flushing. Why? "There are only ten or so of these marshes left in the nation," says Paul, "and we don't have the luxury of waiting with the natural process. Somehow we have to do this eight-hundred-thousand-dollar job within a total park budget of two hundred thousand dollars a year." And this was only Paul's second month on the job!

Still, he has managed to accomplish a great deal toward what the Marine Sanctuaries Act stated as its main goals—research and education. There is a group of citizens in San Diego who came together around their interest in the marsh. They got a grant from the Coastal Conservancy, and together with Paul's help, they are midway through a project to restore nine acres of the marsh to its original condition—clearing out nonnative vegetation, replanting with the native pickleweed and cordgrass, and reopening channels of water that have been closed. When Paul showed me around the estuary, already there was a blue heron diving on a pool of fish where neither one had been seen for years. And therein lies the beauty of the sanctuaries.

If you and your kids want some hands-on experience with the ocean, there are people like Paul at each of California's four sanctuaries to facilitate your participation. You can help with their programs—restoring the habitat, digging in the mudflats for specimens, counting birds, making field observations, drawing animals, writing educational pamphlets—or simply enjoy the beauty on your own.

Chapter 6
God's Country

"God's country" is how the mariners of northern California refer to the waters of the south. The Southern California Bight is how this territory below Point Conception is properly named—all the waters encompassed by the emerald green isles on the outside and the mainland shore, down to the somewhat arbitrary Mexican border to the south. But the long beaches, light breezes, and a saturation sun inspire anything *but* propriety among the people who thrive on its shore.

Fishermen of the north who make sometime forays into the south in pursuit of a school of albacore come back exclaiming with astonishment, "You wouldn't believe it; there're days at a time down there when you can work in an unbuttoned shirt." The mid-Pacific high pressure center that abandons the northern latitudes in the winter months is nearly always in position to protect the south from the intrusion of battering storms. On the rare occasion that a low pressure trough invades the system, there are always the islands to tame the southerly swell before it reaches the beach. And in the spring and summer, when northern waters are being regularly whipped into six-foot, ten-foot, and fifteen-foot seas, the southern waters are protected not only by their lower latitudes but also by the lay of the land. Above Point Conception the coast runs in a north to south direction; below the point, the coast lies more west to east, forming a great natural lee to the prevailing winds and sea—a bight, the Southern California Bight.

Add to this the warm water temperature, six to eight degrees warmer than northern waters, and the inviting, soothing blue hues of the sea, and it's no wonder the people of the south are given to play—Sunday sailing to a hidden cove in the sunny isles, evening walks on the beach, sunbathing on the sand with only the splash of the waves to cover your skin, diving in the forests of kelp, and swimming, just plain swimming (just the thought of it is an act of masochism in the north).

God's country, that's how Ralph Hazard thought of it when he was a young kid in Santa Barbara fishing with his dad, launching their skiff through the quiet of the predawn surf. They headed out to the nearshore beds of kelp and had their lines in the water for the early morning bite of rock cod and sea bass that they fished with a hook and line. And pretty soon they were able to buy a boat with a motor, a slow boat. Now they left from the harbor at two o'clock in the morning so they could get to the middle grounds by dawn. Southern California doesn't have the wind-driven upwelling that is characteristic of northern waters, but there are spots, like the ridges in the middle of the Santa Barbara Channel, where the northward-moving currents are forced to fountain to the surface when they encounter the precipitous underwater terrain. And as in all areas of upwelling, when the nutrients of the bottom are carried to the light on the surface, the plankton blooms explosively and the fishes gather to eat. The ridges in the middle of the Santa Barbara Channel are a fountain of life—rock cod, halibut, mackerel, and sharks. And pretty soon, father and son were able to buy a first-class boat that could take them even farther, to the prolific grounds surrounding the Channel Islands. Here the great kelp beds were nearly pristine and the fishing a primal dream. A great fishery existed throughout the Southern California Bight, making San Pedro harbor south of Los Angeles one of the biggest fishing ports on the whole west coast, a great fishery that supported more different species of marine mammals than any other location in the world.

Nowadays, Ralph Hazard still gets up at two o'clock in the morning and heads his dragger out to the middle grounds of the Santa Barbara Channel to tow for shrimp and prawns. Only now he talks of a nightmare; he calls it "the death of a thousand cuts."

A few years back, an SAS airliner and a United flight went down in Santa Monica Bay on their approach to Los Angeles airport. The airlines asked Ralph to go down to Santa Monica Bay, which had been closed for quite some time to commercial fishing, and drag for wreckage. He couldn't believe what he found. "Did you ever see fish with ulcers?" he asked me, with the shock still fresh in his voice. "The fish we picked up you wouldn't put on the table. They had all kinds of diseases in them—tumors, large blotches, open sores, tails chewed up. It made me sick just to look at these animals. But what do you expect when you dump all the sewage of the city into the place where these animals live? They couldn't pay me enough to ever go dragging there again.

"And then we have that situation down off Pedro, Long Beach, and Orange County. I never go down there any more, but every once in a while a couple of the guys will go to check it out and they don't even stay the whole day. They make one tow, and they're on their way home. There's bed springs, refrigerators, car bodies, and so much garbage over every square inch of bottom there's no way you can work down there. Today, San Pedro is harbor to less than a dozen fishing boats, and most of them fish long distance.

"We don't have much time to be worrying about that, though, because we got a bigger problem right here in our own backyard. We've got oil, and they tell me it's bigger than Alaska. And it wouldn't surprise me a bit, the way they got us coming and going. We've already lost half our grounds just to the garbage they've left on the bottom—the old drill bits, pieces of pipe, cable, and big drums. And when we try to get compensation, Exxon says, 'No way.' They say we haven't lost anything, and besides, they say if they set a precedent with us, then everyone will jump in and want compensation for lost pleasure grounds and everything else. Now they're starting drilling operations at the high reef at the middle grounds. And that's where I work.

"There's a large, flat shallow area between Ventura and Anacapa Island. The English sole come through there every year to feed on the worms that live on the bottom. When they had the oil spill back in 1963, they sunk the oil with heavy earth. It covered the bottom and smothered it. It killed off all the little worms that the English were living on. It took over three years before the bottom came back at all and the English came through again. And when they did come through, they were real skinny, and their tails were all beat up, and they wouldn't stay. They went right on through. It's just in the last year that the worms have come back. And the oil companies say, 'Prove it.'

"But we're not Ph.D.'s and the oil companies know that, and they know that the biologists don't get involved in something like that. There's no grants for it, so they don't see it. It's very, very aggravating. Do you want me to go on?

"The seismic boats don't use dynamite anymore, so there's no more dead fish coming up. But they still use explosions. They have air guns on a one-to-two-mile cable that they tow behind the boat. They chase the fish away. It's just like getting kicked in the stomach—boom, boom, boom, every three minutes. You'll be fishing halibut and doing pretty well, and a geophysical boat will come through and the fishing will drop down to nothing. Then three days later it will start to come back. You know what the oil companies say? They say, 'Prove it.'

"There's no way of stopping them. If the oil's there, they're going to get it. We're just trying to slow them down a little and make them more careful—like no garbage. But the meetings are always the same go around and nothing done. But you watch," said Ralph, with all the sunshine and hope he has stored from growing up in God's country, "we're seven large draggers and five smaller ones, and between the twelve of us we're taking on Exxon." And he laughed.

Chapter 7

Under the Golden Gate

Nothing suggests infinite serenity more than a path of moonlight stretched from the horizon to the shore across a nighttime sea. Nothing is more subtle than the tide's almost imperceptible climbing and receding on the pilings of a dock or the slope of a shore, a slow and gentle pulse generated by the quiet pull of the moon. And nothing is more deceptive. The tides of California rarely exceed eight feet and are actually unremarkable compared with tides in other parts of the world. But even here, the tides work events in the sea of such magnitude and savagery that volcanoes, earthquakes, and floods all harnessed together couldn't make a whisper to the tidal roar. Not only in the ferocity of the moment, but in sheer persistence too, only the movements of the tides can keep pace with the relentless push of time. Many of these events are hidden beneath the surface of the sea, but there are places where they emerge, visible in their full fury even to one standing on the shore. In California, the show is nowhere more dramatic than under the Golden Gate.

All of California has what are called semidiurnal tides. This means that there are two sets of high and low water every day, with one of these sets being smaller than the other in amplitude. This tidal pattern, in fact, is the norm around the whole Pacific rim, and it is the pattern that is closest to what would be expected under the ideal conditions of an earth completely covered with water. This is true, of course, because the Pacific is the largest body of water in the world. It's a rhythm that results from the superimposition of the moon wave, with a period of just under twelve hours, and the sun wave, with a period of exactly twelve hours. The major variations in our tide can be explained by the relative positions of the sun, the moon, and the earth.

Since the positions and orbits of these bodies are themselves very predictable, you would probably guess that there is a big computer back at the National Ocean Survey in Washington that takes all this orbital data, mulls it over, sums up the vectors; then once a year, when someone pushes the button, out pop the tide books. Well, there is a computer, and true, it pumps out the tide books once a year, but how it does this isn't much more sophisticated than the way in which the farmer's almanac is prepared. Because they still can't predict the tides from the theory. There are many more variables involved, such as the lay of the land, that are as yet too unwieldy for the computer, and others, like barometric pressure, that are too unpredictable. So what this computer does all year is swallow volumes upon volumes of empirical data on the measured tide heights for all the years past, from all parts of the coast, average them out, and match them with similar orbital conditions of the past; it then publishes a best guess. The most sophisticated theory involved is that in any given geographical location, nature is likely to repeat itself.

So next time you whip out your tide book to auger your fishing trip, your dive, or a trip to the beach, keep in mind that it's just like any other bible; if you live according to the book without constantly checking in on reality, the effects can be far worse than embarrassing.

Nowhere on the coast are the tidal vagaries more exaggerated and magnified than in San Francisco Bay. This is mostly due to its unique kidney shape, with the narrow entrance to the sea situated halfway down its length. Twice a day, the tide enters (and leaves) the bay through its one-mile-wide mouth to raise the levels of water over the 400-square-mile body anywhere from two to nine feet. The volumes of water involved are so great that, if the Golden Gate were a river, it would have the highest volume flow of any river in the world. And as all that rush of water roars its way through the irregularity of islands, gorges, banks, and hair-pin turns, the result is a raging, unpredictable broil on a scale that can grab a net attached to a sixty-foot boat and pull the whole works into one of its eddies like a leaf being whisked into a storm drain.

In the south bay, the tide sloshes like water in a pan, creating high-water levels two feet above average at the tip of the bay, then reflecting back, creating a standing wave with a node halfway down the bay. In the north bay, the quiet moon hurls the water straight up out of the deep channels onto the flats like a mammoth waterfall in reverse, all the while doing battle with the currents of the outgoing tide that isn't yet complete; it broils and eddies around the islands and funnels through the narrow straits where it is forced to ferocious speed by the insistent push of the water coming in behind it. And everywhere there are massive vertical and horizontal eddies and flash floods that run countercurrent — all of it forming and disappearing, snaking and submerging, at times in less than a minute. Stand underneath the Golden Gate at Fort Baker during a maximum ebb, and even just looking at the action on the surface, I guarantee you'll be impressed.

The tide books? Sometimes they're off by as much as two hours; sometimes slack water never even occurs throughout a full cycle of the tide. Local knowledge? The people who have operated vessels on this water their whole lives live by the same rule: the exception is what to expect.

If your mind has been changed about the peaceful swell of the tide, consider the surprise of Captain John Maddox, experienced master of the 127-foot tugboat *Sentinel*, with 9,000 horsepower, one of the most powerful oceangoing tugs on the sea. December 31, 1979, it was embarking on a routine run from Oakland to Honolulu with two 100-foot barges, 6,000 tons each. They've been doing it for years, and these days it's nothing, what with the double-drum motors and surge chains and adjustable brakes. The transcript of the Coast Guard investigation said there was no concern among the crew that night as the *Sentinel* left the pier in Oakland and headed for the Golden Gate. The weather conditions didn't have the makings of a Sunday cruise, but the predicted waves still wouldn't even wash the windows of a tug like the *Sentinel*. Once under the Gate they headed out to the southwest, the same course taken by every other large vessel to ensure a safe crossing of the bar.

It is foolhardy to say which is the worst place on the ocean, because the ocean changes more with time than with place. But then again the bars aren't really all ocean; they're half ocean and half land. And therein lies their treachery. The bar is a shallow shoal of sediment laid by fast-moving water entering the sea. The energy and motion of free rolling waves on the open sea reach deep into the water to depths that are many times their height. They roll in great circular unimpeded motions across the vast plains of the sea. But where the waves and the bar meet, the tremendous energy in the wave's bottom half is walled and pushed into the top half of the wave.

A crew member testified at the investigation about the conditions they met on the bar outside the gate:

> I was getting pretty concerned, because the swells were getting big. Then finally, about four o'clock, the skipper said he wasn't making much headway. He was working out, but he was having some problems getting her back out in the channel, or in between the buoys. Then about four o'clock, there were several very large waves. I'll tell you, it's absolutely the worst bar conditions I have ever seen. I have never seen anything quite like it in my career and I have crossed bars many times. . . . I just couldn't tell you—I mean I wouldn't—we were looking up at waves. Now, I don't know how high those would be, but it's pretty high when your wheel house is twenty-two feet and you're looking up.

All the other crew members who testified at the investigation said that the waves encountered by the *Sentinel* on the bar were between thirty-five and forty feet high.

The next morning the citizens of Marin County woke up to radio announcements of a possible evacuation because two barges that had broken from the *Sentinel* were being smashed on the headlands and were threatening to spew forth chlorine gas. The leak disaster was averted, but the Coast Guard wanted very much to know how this had happened. They especially wanted to know about those waves, because a boat crossing the bar two hours before the *Sentinel* and another crossing a few hours later had reported only twelve- to fifteen-foot swells called for on the VHF weather. It's true that the *Sentinel* had crossed the bar on the maximum ebb of the tide, and it's well known that the outgoing run of water does as much to distort the waves as the shoal of the bar itself; but this ebb was only a small one, 2.3 knots by the book.

It's as impossible to say exactly what conditions were encountered that night on the bar as it is for the tide books to accurately predict the tide. But on the day of December 31, and for a week before, the Bay Area was being battered by a series of southerly storms. With a severe low pressure system, it's not unusual for the tides on the bay to be raised by two feet over the prediction, just because there isn't enough air pressure to hold them down. That makes a lot more water to be dumped on the outgoing tide, not to mention all the added runoff from the swollen rivers, or all the other unknowns that come under the spell of the moon, the silent rogue in the sea.

Chapter 8

The San Francisco Bay Model

Instruments for probing the mysteries of the sea are being revo-
lutionized daily. But one of the most attractive methods, because
of its logical simplicity and its availability to everyone, is to build
a model, fill it up with water, turn on the tides, and make your
measurements.

The U.S. Army Corps of Engineers has over sixty acres of land
in Vicksburg, Mississippi, housing models of all the major water
systems and harbors in the United States. The one exception is San
Francisco Bay. The reason for this is that there already was a
model of the bay located in Sausalito. The model is built of
cement; it's accurate to the contours of the bay; and it covers an

impressive area the size of two football fields. It was built in 1956 by the Army Corps of Engineers to test the Reber plan. John Reber was a producer of amateur theatricals. His greatest production was an emotional one-man oratory proclaiming the virtues of his plan to build two mammoth dams in the approximate positions of the present-day San Francisco to Oakland bridge and the Richmond–San Rafael bridge. The purpose was to create two large bodies of fresh water at either end of the bay for the enhancement of recreation and agriculture. He presented this plan to so many clubs, granges, churches, and civic groups that it soon gained widespread support. Congress decreed that the Army Corps use the model to determine if this plan would have a deleterious effect on the bay. (To the ear of the 1980s this sounds a little like asking if a tire will go flat if you let the air out.) Their study put the Reber plan to rest once and for all.

Since that time, the Army Corps has used the model for studying many aspects of the bay, from the flushing of pollutants to the effects of filling in the wetlands. Most recently, the model has been focused on a question that is eerily reminiscent of its first charge. What are the effects on the bay of diverting the fresh water of the Sacramento River system down to Los Angeles. To answer this, the Army Corps has just completed construction of an addition to the model that includes the river deltas.

One criticism of such a model as a research tool is that its simplicity of logic is frequently not far enough away from simplistic. For example, one very important question, which concerns almost every proposed project, is what percentage of bay water is exchanged (or flushed by the tides). Just how exasperating this has proven to be is indicated by the fact that, after numerous and intensive studies using every method available, the answer given by scientists ranges between 10 and 80 percent. Your child could have come up with that at the breakfast table.

So why not put a dye in the model, pump through a couple of tides, and simply measure how much of the dye is left? "Oh, you can do that all right," says John Sustar, a scientist at the model, "but the problem is that the answer you get will be wrong. Because in the real bay, when the tide goes out, some of the water that goes out to sea returns to the bay on the next tide. So, at the very least, we'd have to add a section to the model that includes the current system right outside the Gate."

And then, one wonders, in order to recreate the currents outside the Gate, would you need to extend the model to include the California Current? It's ironic; simple logic may eventually take us to the conclusion that you need a model the size of the Pacific in order to answer even the most simple questions about the bay. And then you're right back where you started.

Perhaps one of the most important contributions of the model is coming out of a little side project that was begun a few years back. The bay model has always been open a few hours a week to the curious public. But four years ago, the Army Corps took some of its recreation funds and turned the model into a park. Now there is a lively turnover of exhibits, lectures, classes, slide shows: a great program free for all, with a knowledgeable staff ready to answer questions on topics and issues concerning the bay—and the magnificent model of the bay is at the center of it all.

Chapter 9

San Francisco Bay

Stand on a Marin hill looking across the bay toward Richmond, and you will see oil refineries framed by islands and straits in front and the hills of Richmond behind. Look out from the shores of Oakland toward the shipyards of Hunters Point, and vast plains of shallow tidelands swallow the steel in their sweeping expanse. Even looking straight into the guts of its commerce, the beauty of San Francisco Bay is persistent. And though pressed by four million people on its shores, there are views around the bay's full perimeter that are as breathtaking as the pristine vistas of the most exotic lands of the world.

Even as it absorbs drainage from the towns and the ships and

docks of their trade, the bay teems with all kinds of fish and birds
of a hundred different habitats, from freshwater to marine, from
rocky nesting places to dark muddy holes in deep channels,
marshlands and kelp beds, mudflats and sandy shoals—web upon
web of life, one around the bend from the next. Nearly every fish
from the ocean comes into the bay at one time or another in an
ever-changing cycle. Dangle a hook off a city dock, and you can
catch salmon, halibut, bass, flounder, sturgeon, perch, rock cod,
a dozen kinds of shark; over a hundred species of fish live in or
visit the bay. Such great schools of anchovies and herring come
into the bay that commercial fishermen can wrap upwards of a
hundred tons in the set of a net.

The ocean of the northern California coast has a mean reputation, it's true, but the San Francisco Bay is a recreationist's paradise. It can be rowed, cruised, and sailed at leisure, yet it's never
so tame as to bore your senses. The roaring tides and changing
winds, the curl of the fog, the surge from the sea beyond will challenge your hundredth cruise. When you need to get away, there
are a thousand hideaways—coves and inlets nestled from the
wind where you can party or bask alone in the sun. If you're
broke and need to impress a visitor from out of town, there's the
bay in all its showy splendor.

It would be easy to go on with all the particulars of how,
when, and where to enjoy the bay, but it hardly seems necessary.
Look out over the water any day of the week, any time of night or
day, and you could hardly envision a more persuasive argument
for including people in the family of marine mammals, so thor-
oughly have the citizens occupied its every niche. In fact, it was
the citizens of the bay, not the leaders, scientists, politicians, or
engineers, who were the first to recognize that the incredible
vitality, the kaleidoscopic beauty of the bay was in trouble. It was
the beachcombers, hikers, sailors—alias secretaries, plumbers,
grocers—who set out to save their bay with an idea that was
unique to the country at the time and has since become the basis
for the most progressive ocean legislation in the nation.

San Francisco Bay is bordered by nine counties, and as they
are for most other bodies of water, including the ocean, decisions
about the bay's development were made piecemeal and indepen-
dently by each town government for the shoreline bordering its

town. It was as erroneous a concept, thought the people of the bay, as believing that the sun revolved around the earth. A vast diversity of citizens' groups were concerned about the consequences of continuing in this manner. Number one among their concerns was that 37 percent of the bay had already been lost to the commercial quest for more land. It was diked, filled, and developed, and even more ambitious plans were in the steamroller stage, ready to finish the job, to fill this shallow estuary in its entirety, save for the deep water channels needed so ships of commerce could pass.

In a great coordinating effort, these citizens' groups put a referendum on the state ballot to form a temporary commission to prepare a plan to protect the bay. Yet another commission, you say? It is true, but in 1969 when the plan was submitted to the state, the commission was made a permanent state agency, the Bay Conservation and Development Commission, with full regulatory authority over filling and dredging within all tidal areas of the bay. Any project inconsistent with the bay plan is not allowed.

What is unique about BCDC is its 27-member commission: nine county representatives, four city representatives, five state officials, seven citizens, and two federal representatives.

For the first time, it was recognized that a body of water must be governed regionally, as a whole, based on the novel understanding that what happens at one end of a bathtub will quickly be felt at the other.

Coincidentally, this bay plan comprised the first comprehensive study of the bay. How such a study could have been neglected in an area blessed with some of the great universities and research facilities in the world is a fascinating story. Biologist Joel Hedgepeth explains how it happens in his introduction to a recent symposium called San Francisco Bay the Urbanized Estuary. He tells how by the late 1930s when the decision was made to build Shasta Dam, it was thought that the rivers were barren of fish, and he tells of frustrated biologists from the Department of Fish and Game trying to convince the University of California at Berkeley that somebody in California *had* to teach a course on fish. Prior to this last decade, the marine environment was considered inconsequential.

BCDC has grown to establish policies and initiate studies on a wide variety of subjects relating to the bay, from its climate to its microbes, but much of the time at bimonthly meetings is spent in laborious consideration of permit applications.

"But look what it's accomplished," says staff engineer Bob Millikin. "In the past three years we've restored more acres of the bay than we've developed. And the way we do this is primarily by mitigation. For example, before we granted construction permits on the Dumbarton Bridge, the builders had to donate eighty acres of refuge on the east side of the bay."

"The same general idea as the California Coastal Commission," I said, in complete ignorance of the history of the bay that provided my living and recreation for over a decade.

"Wait a minute," said Bob, quick to correct me. "You're like most people who think that BCDC was modeled on the Coastal Commission, but it was the other way around."

Phil Williams is the bay hydrologist for BCDC. His office is on the waterfront, hanging precariously over the brink of the problem he has to solve: subsidence! BCDC may have stopped the filling, but it has no more jurisdiction over the consequences of past filling than it has over the outgoing tide. Nonetheless, subsidence, the shrinking, sinking, and flooding of the earth that was placed in the bay as fill, is a problem inherited by the commission and citizens alike. "All the buildings are cracking, the drainage systems are buckling, the dikes are breaking, and the maintenance costs are increasing," says Phil. "These problems take about thirty years to develop, and we're just seeing the beginning of it. And it's the taxpayer who picks up the bill, because the speculators have walked and the builders are long gone."

Dealing with this mess is especially frustrating because once again there is an urgent threat to the entire life of the bay, more sinister by its invisibility, more pervasive in its effect than even the destruction of tidelands by fill. And this time the PR is good, and this time the people are fighting without the data they need— because nobody in California wanted to teach about fish.

The heart of the problem is that San Francisco Bay is an estuary, like Mission Bay, Tomales Bay, Humboldt Bay, like the mouth of every river that empties into the sea. Estuaries are the most productive areas on earth, nourishing more growth per acre than the rain forests of the tropics or the most fertilized wheat field of the plains. The mudflats and marshes produce a brackish microbial brew that is ideal for young larval fish and crustaceans, and a great number of marine species have evolved to come into the estuary to spawn or, like the salmon and striped bass, the young move in shortly after they've hatched. The estuaries are truly the nurseries to the sea. And in California, compared to the east coast, they are few and far between.

Characteristic of every estuary is exposure to the sea on one end and a river that enters from behind. For a long time the river was seen as having a rather passive role in the life of the estuary, merely supplying the fresh water to maintain the reduced salinity that is so favorable to the growth of the small organisms. But now we understand that the river is no less than the estuary's lifeblood, providing the nutrients it has leached from the forest and plains. At the same time, it is primary in flushing the estuary of the waste accumulated by so much life. Without the river, the estuary would quickly stagnate and die.

The tides, which for a long time were thought to be responsible for flushing, are now understood to have little more than a sloshing action. It is the same as if you were to breathe through a very long tube—breathe as hard as you can, and still you would only be inhaling the same stale air that you exhaled on the last breath. It's due to the lack of a river that the south end of the bay, though its tides are higher than the north's, takes triple the time to flush.

One more important phenomenon of every estuary is the "null zone." It's where the upward press of the sea equals the downward press of the river, and all the sediments and nutrients are trapped as in a miniature sargasso sea. Whereas life in the rest of the estuary is merely superabundant, life in the null zone is teeming— millions of young fish feed and grow on the vast schools of shrimp and dense crops of plankton. The null zone is a fisherman's paradise, where he can prey on the predators that come here to gorge on the young. A fisherman in San Francisco Bay used to go somewhere between the Gate and the Delta to locate this incredible sphere of life; now the null zone fluctuates somewhere between

Suisun Bay and Carquinez Strait, and if things keep going as they are, the null zone will soon be pushed up into the confined space of the Sacramento River, where there won't be room for the extensive blooms that are needed to feed the fish. What's going on, of course, is that the Sacramento River system is being diverted to the south and the estuary is bleeding to death.

Two years ago, construction of the costly Peripheral Canal was voted down by a resounding 95 percent of California voters. Many people thought they were dealing a death blow to the diversion of water south, such is the insidiousness of sophisticated publicity. In actuality, the Peripheral Canal was merely a change of plumbing. Many of the developers themselves were against it, and some of the fisheries people were actually for it because of the strict conservation measures riding along with the bill. The important fact is that even before the canal was proposed, 50 percent of the Sacramento River was already being diverted, and every year that percentage is increasing, with or without the Peripheral Canal. Currently, there are four alternative plans for diverting more of the Sacramento flow, each one of them more destructive to the estuary than the canal itself, and none of them is ever likely to come before a vote of the citizens. Back in the committees, the developers argue endlessly that the estuaries' need for fresh water cannot be proved. And it's true—there has been so little study of this intricate system, of the lives of its fishes, of the dynamics of the bay itself, that the numbers and statistics needed to move the machinery simply do not exist.

Phil Williams tells of another hydrologist who came here to this country four years ago. "He took one look at our situation, all the arguing back and forth, and he said, 'Hey, guys, you better take a look at what happened elsewhere in the world—the destruction of the estuary and the whole Black Sea fisheries because of water diversion there. There's nothing to argue about.' The fisheries people have been saying these things for a long time," says Phil, "but they're not in charge here, the engineers are.

"Well, I'll tell you," he continued. "I know how to stop this thing right now. All the problems of California water could be solved if you started charging agribusiness a fair price for the water. They're the main users; they consume a full 85 percent of

California water, and it's the taxpayer who pays for it. If agribusiness had to pay for the water they use, they'd start conserving it and changing their cropping plans, and we wouldn't even be discussing this.

"You know, the food they're growing down there isn't going for the starving masses; if they were serious about that they would be growing very different crops—crops that don't need that kind of water. Did you know that most of the water is going down there to irrigate pastureland for cattle? If they had to pay for that water, those cattle would overnight be back in the Midwest where they belong."

Phil's a busy man; he was eager to get right back to a deskful of dilemmas—cracking buildings, sinking lands, breaking dikes—the debris from developers past. "Look," he said as I started to leave, "there are a lot of people around here who are concerned about the bay—don't get me wrong—but they're not being heard, because in decision making it's the water exporters who have the power." Perhaps though, I thought, the same beachcombers, hikers, and sailors—alias secretaries, plumbers, and grocers—will brew up another innovative plan that will work just as well as the last.

Chapter 10

Between Pacific Tides

Overdue debts, the check's not in the mail; the deadline's way
behind you, and the work is still in front; the cops come home
with your kid, and your boyfriend sends a note that asks, "Have I
neglected to mention that I'm married with three kids?" You could
pop a few pills, or head for parts unknown, or call a friend, or
even shoot yourself. But a lot of people find their solace at the
beach.

They say it recharges their batteries. Personally, I think it's
more like fixing a magnet that's been so jarred, nicked, pocked,
and dropped that all its polarized particles are pointing every
which way but north. The only way to help that magnet is to put

it in the presence of a force bigger than itself. Set it in the field of a bigger magnet, and all the disoriented particles flip back into position and are once again coherent. What bigger magnet than the ocean? You feel things lining up in their proper perspective as soon as you reach the shore.

Duxbury Reef in Bolinas is the spot I've gone back to again and again for fifteen years. Not only can you walk up to the shore, but when the tide is out you can keep on going, meandering over the bottom of the sea, malingering with the starfish, looking at the urchins, and thinking, life can be very different indeed. It's hard to say just what these sea creatures do for me, or for all the other people who put red circles in their tide book around the days of the minus tides so as not to miss a chance to stare into the pools.

Duxbury Reef is the largest on a coast of many reefs, too many to list here. They're everywhere, except where there's a sandy beach. And the most pristine are the ones that have never been put on a list. The special beauty of Duxbury is its multiplicity of forms —mudflats full of burrowing clams and shrimps, protected rocky areas, eelgrass flats, and open coast rocky shores where the water comes and leaves the gorges and pools in an ever-changing array of rivers, waterfalls, and lakes. And everywhere the most intriguing shapes, and colors, and activities of life abound.

Alice in all of Wonderland never encountered such strange ones as these. I've never made much of an effort to get to know their names or their times and place of birth. They've been something magical to stare at to forget the stresses on land. Yet over time some things become obvious. These eloquently simple creatures live in the most stressful environment on earth. One hour they're baking in the hot sun; their pools evaporate and become as saline as the Great Salt Lake. The next hour they're being pounded by vicious surf, and an hour after that, they're submerged in a cold and darkened sea with giant fish rooting around for a meal. And in the course of a day the ocean can sweep in a sandbar and smother the colonies in sand. But as far as who eats whom and how, and who spawns when and where, I had only an idle guess.

It seemed as though I ought to at least educate myself a bit more before writing of this other world. The libraries and bookstores have no end of choices on life in the tide pools, books filled with copious illustrations and vital statistics, but none of them drew me in. Especially not the "bible," *Between Pacific Tides*. This one looked too heavy to even pull off the shelf. I had seen it for years and always passed it by. Then a couple of weeks ago I checked it out of the library and have been lost to browsing it ever since.

The authors themselves are a fascinating lot. Ed Ricketts was John Steinbeck's friend. Steinbeck immortalized him in *Cannery Row* as Doc, the philosopher–tide pool collector who made his living selling specimens to laboratories and schools. Steinbeck also wrote the introduction to the first edition of *Between Pacific Tides*, which was printed back in 1939. John Calvin, the second author, has a printing business in Alaska. He never was a zoologist. In fact, Ed Ricketts never graduated from college either. Joel Hedgepeth, responsible for the latest revision of the book, is a marine biologist who currently lives in Santa Rosa and should be named a state treasure for all he has done for our sea. Not only for his boundless curiosity in exploring its mysteries, but for his teaching and his willingness to get involved in the politics and the philosophy, for his incredible breadth of vision in an area that increasingly fosters specialization.

Together they have produced a book that presents the shore intact with its magic. Thousands of animals and plants are portrayed, each in a different light, amid explanations of the oceanography affecting them, with the stories of those people who studied them, and unashamed of conjecture, with threads and filaments reaching back into history and across the world without ever leaving the pools. *Between Pacific Tides* doesn't make you feel as though you're on a field trip being led by the teacher; it speaks to your intelligence and to your boundless curiosity. The illustrations are the best that exist, the appendixes exhaustive, and the annotated bibliography the most extensive that I've seen. In one book, the whole west coast shore, in all its dimensions and magnetism, solace and sensations, can be brought into your home for delving in the magic as needed.

Chapter 11

Cape Mendocino

Cape Mendocino (between Shelter Cove and Eureka) is a naked, mountainous fist of land that punches farther west into the sea than any other point of land in the continental United States, and the ocean punches back. The currents boil and the sea winds clash with the land "breezes" that rush down the mountains at a frisky little pace that not infrequently exceeds a hundred miles an hour. The sea conditions are most often what the forecasters call "confused," because the wave patterns are coming from more than one direction at once; the fishermen call these conditions "jackass" because of the unmistakable character of the ride you get. And every once in a while two of these waves come together at just the right angle and explode into the sum of their parts, forming what's known as a freak wave, which has all the grace and curve of a brick wall. Freak waves are reported in many ocean areas, but Cape Mendocino, cursed as it is with the extreme impulses of so many forces, seems to be their favorite spawning ground.

This cape is no less intense below the surface. The deep underwater canyons and immense upwellings of the area produce vertical and horizontal rivers that know no banks. Like rogues, they snake on ever-changing courses through the territory. As they move along the surface of the sea, they, too, alter the shapes of the waves, sharpening them suddenly into the vicious forms of the bar. In a matter of minutes, the shift of a river can churn the seas into an unforgiving hell. The nearest shelter, Shelter Cove or Eureka, is five or six hours either way, and only God can get you there.

You would think that every boat coming through here would be aggressively pursuing its course to someplace else. But the intense upwelling and stirring currents frequently make the waters off Cape Mendocino a gigantic feedlot for thousands and thousands of albacore and salmon. You make a trip to the cape and you stand an even chance of coming out with either $10,000 worth of fish or $10,000 worth of damage. So the fishermen hang on the anchor in the cove or tie to the docks at Eureka and wait for the weather to break. The problem is that you can never predict what the weather's going to be in a different spot; all you can know is the conditions where you're at. And even then the wind may be pegging your gauge at seventy knots and the weather reports are calling it five.

Captain Edward Harrison sees it differently. The Fleet Numerical Weather Service located at the Naval Postgraduate School in Monterey houses one of the most sophisticated computers in the world. Its sole function is predicting marine weather. Captain Harrison offered to show me around. But first he made me a cup of coffee and explained that this computer is constantly taking in data from satellites, ships, airplanes, and floating automatic buoys from every country in the world, including Russia and China. "How come the predictions are almost always wrong?" I asked, without a lot of tact.

"They're not," he answered, "unless you're talking about local conditions."

"But aren't all conditions local?"

And he explained: "The theory on predicting ocean weather is complete. It's the three laws of thermodynamics. That's all you need to know. After that it's only a question of resolution. Right now we can predict the weather over a broad area, and all that's needed is more data to tighten down on the parameters."

"But isn't that like saying that if you know the nature of a nerve impulse and the circuitry, you could predict a person's thoughts?"

"Exactly!"

I figured that he didn't understand my point, so I continued. "Even though it's possible to mathematically describe the electronic forces in the hydrogen and oxygen atom, the computer still can't predict the boiling point of water."

"That's just the same problem, a problem of resolution; you add sophistication to the system and you get closer and closer to the answer."

We were both puzzled and intrigued enough by what the other was trying to say that we continued like this for half an hour.

"You know about the computer that edits books? The one that does things like take all the passive verbs and make them active, to make it grammatically more correct? When they put *Moby Dick* through the computer it came out flat as a pancake. In other words, when you tighten down on the parameters it seems to me you lose the quirks that make it work."

"I don't know *Moby Dick*," he said, realizing we'd had enough. "Why don't you let me show you around."

We passed through a couple of doors and security clearances and entered a huge room that was as dustless as a spaceship. There were row upon row of large rectangular cases with neither markings nor dials on the front, side, or back. Aside from this, the room was empty. "This is it," he said, with an air of paternal pride. "There's more updated information on the ocean weather in here than exists anywhere in the world."

I couldn't help but wonder if we were talking about the same ocean. Where was the unexpected that is the earmark of the meeting of such forces, the winds that whip around the compass without warning or mercy, the sudden upwellings that churn the rhythmic seas into chaos, and the reckless urge to tempt it all? How could there be such opposite visions, without a link of intersection, on something as big and imposing as the sea?

Captain Harrison then walked me over to the two largest units, each about the size of three refrigerators. "These are the brains of the outfit," he said, looking up. "They contain the theory of the ocean and coordinate all the rest of the computers here."

And there finally was the link. Written in huge white letters across the face of the brains were their names, Bonnie and Clyde, his rudder and his helm, the epitome of wanton impulsiveness and lawless disregard.

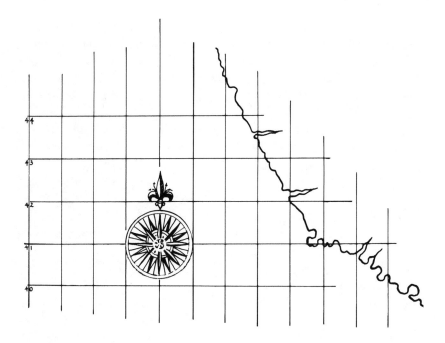

Chapter 12

Reading the Ocean

What at first glance seems to be a giant, drab poster of lines and numbers actually contains more fascinating information about the sea than any printed text. And with just a little practice in reading them, ocean charts allow you to visualize the sea in its hidden dimensions—all that lies beyond your eyes. Naturally, these charts are indispensable to the mariner, but just because you choose to enjoy the ocean from the security of terra firma or the near-shore waters, don't make the mistake of thinking these charts are useless to you. If you fish, dive, surf, tide-pool, hike, or hunt with binoculars, a chart will put you on the spot.

First of all, the chart gives you the depth of the water over the entire ocean bottom, a wealth of data that has some rather obvious ramifications. You don't throw an anchor rigged with fifty feet of line into a hundred feet of water; nor would you want to set off on a lyrical cruise to a four-fathom shoal when the sea is running a ten-foot swell. But these numbers dotting the chart have a more subtle value as well. They form a picture of the underwater terrain, its geography. Canyons, ledges, escarpments, sea mounts, gorges, and plateaus pop out in bas relief for someone with the most minimal experience in perusing charts. This visualization is greatly facilitated by the fact that on many charts points of equal depth are connected by a line, producing an image similar to the contour lines on a weather map. So? So, if you go down to a long stretch of beach and throw your line randomly into the water, that's probably what you'll catch, the proverbial random fish. But if you take a look at the chart and you see a little canyon coming up to one section of the beach, you might figure on a little upwelling stirring some action. Or if you see a ledge that's positioned to stonewall the current, you might want to consider the bait that's getting trapped in the broil. The geography of the bottom determines the behavior of the water to a great extent and provides a wealth of clues, not only to the best fishing spots, but also the best locations for surf breaks, bird flocks, and diving. The difficult part is giving educated guesses about the relationships between the geography, the tides, the currents, the animals, and the activity you wish to pursue—which process is otherwise referred to as the challenge of the sea. The beauty of this challenge is that it can probably never be reduced to a formula; but unless you have that initial vital information, so easily obtained, it's like looking into the wrong side of a mirror.

Charts also give equally useful information about the character of the bottom! Is it grassy, coral, clay, hard, soft, sticky? Are there offshore reefs, breakers, washrocks? You may not see this information at first, as it is coded in very tiny letters, but on the blank area of the chart depicting land, the coded abbreviations are explained in full.

The navigational systems and aids coded into these charts are quite complex and are not outlined here as they are of little use to the nonmariner. Besides, anyone planning to go to sea better have

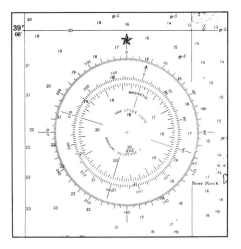

more than a passing acquaintance with them. One aspect of the navigational system, however, can be extremely valuable to the landsman. This is the compass rose. The first thing you are certain to notice about the compass rose is that there are two compasses, one inside the other. This is not done to portray the ambivalence of the human condition or the dialectic of plotting a course. It merely reflects that the true north pole is not located in the same spot as the magnetic north pole. Since the needle of your compass points to the magnetic north, it's the inner circle on the compass rose that you use for determining directions from the chart. There are many reasons you might want to know this; for example, a cove with a northwest exposure will provide very different cover than a cove with a southwest exposure, with regard to wind, current, tide, and light. The same variables will apply, of course, for reefs, rocks, and shoals.

The whole world ocean is plotted on charts. Some are less accurate than others; in fact, relying on charts in some parts of the world is courting disaster. Even off the coast of California, there are any number of unmarked high spots and deviations, though these are not significant unless you're dragging heavy gear. For over-the-water navigation, have no fear, California charts are extremely accurate. And for any given area on the coast you can get four or five different magnifications of the same zone. It is worth repeating, the more you refer to these charts, the more the information is going to come together in your mind with other observations you've made in the area and develop into a multi-dimensional visualization that allows you to be down there without ever getting wet.

Charts are only one of the ocean publications put out regularly and cheaply by the government. Tide books are probably the most familiar, as they are available next to nearly every cash register along the coast. There are two kinds of tide books. The rarer kind includes not only the times of high and low water but also the times of slack, maximum ebb, maximum flood, and their velocities. This is the one to get hold of if possible, you just have to look around. You have to beware of tide tables, unlike charts, and use them only as a guide.

The *Coast Pilot* is a book produced annually by the government for the coastwise navigator. Its contents are gathered and updated from the seamen who regularly cruise our coast. The *Coast Pilot* describes in great detail everything and anything that might catch the human eye while looking into the coast from out at sea. Its purpose, of course, is to assist you in pinpointing your location by visual reference to the land, but its prose and perspective are so unique that you can while away many an hour flipping through its pages.

Anyone who has left home on a bright, hot sunny day for a picnic at the beach and arrived to find conditions too cold and foggy to open the car window knows that marine weather along the coast is quite different from what's taking place even an eighth of a mile inshore. To find out about wind and sea conditions for numerous locations along the coast, as well as a detailed weather synopsis and forecast, monitor the marine weather service broadcasts continually on the weather channel of the VHF radio. This information is updated every four hours.

With the advent of satellites, new data streams are pouring into ground stations, and portions of the information are beginning to be published and distributed for ocean users. One of the early and most dramatic examples of this is the infrared satellite picture of our coast taken at irregular intervals over the sea. The infrared part of the spectrum registers the radiant component of heat; what you get is a vivid picture of relative water temperatures showing the large-scale eddies, plumes, and rips of cold water and their edges. These pictures potentially are extremely useful to the commercial fleet because fish tend to gather at these edges. So far, however, because these conditions change so rapidly and the pictures take so long to be distributed, they remain just interesting data for hindsight and post mortems.

Most of the materials mentioned above, and much more, can usually be obtained at a marine store or coast guard facility. If you can't find what you need, the best approach is to pick up the phone and call your local marine extension agent. These numbers are listed in the Marine Directory at the end of this book.

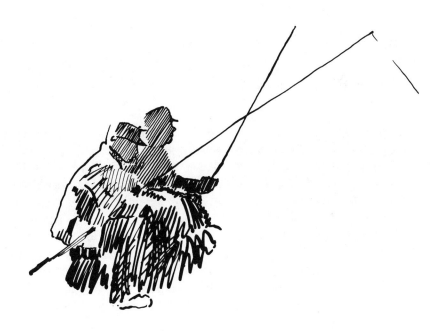

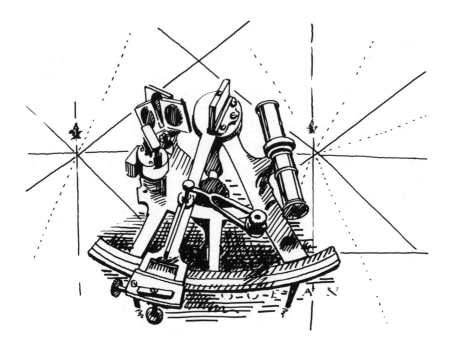

Chapter 13

The Sailor's Workplace

This carpenter of the Pequod *was singularly efficient in those thousand nameless mechanical emergencies continually recurring in a large ship. . . . For not to speak of his readiness in ordinary duties: repairing stove boats, sprung spars, reforming the shape of clumsy-bladed oars, inserting bull's eyes in the deck, or new tree-nails in their side planks . . . he was moreover unhesitatingly expert in all manner of conflicting aptitudes. . . . A lost land-bird of strange plumage strays on board, and is made a captive; out of clean shaved rods of right-whale bone, and cross beams of sperm whale ivory, the carpenter makes a pagoda-looking cage for it. An oarsman sprains his wrist: the carpenter concocts a soothing lotion. Stubb longed for vermillion stars to be painted upon the blade of his every oar; screwing each oar in his big vise of wood, the carpenter symmetrically supplies the constellation.*

Herman Melville, *Moby Dick*

It's been awhile since they tacked up a posting for a ship's carpenter in the big hall at the Sailor's Union. And if Melville's carpenter happened to find himself shipped on a modern-day run, it is doubtful that he would ever once be called to task, from here to the Java Sea. He could spend the entire crossing in awe of refrigeration, autopilots, and satellite navigation, of warm, dry bunks in the after part of the ship, and then return to the beach with a check that would roll him for weeks. It's gotten real downtown in the vessels that ply the sea.

The problem over at the hall is that it's a long time between postings of any jobs at all. And the problem out at sea? Well, it's a far, foreign cry from the gripes of sailors past.

Where are you from? San Francisco? L.A.? San Diego? Have you ever been down to the docks? Ships as big as buildings cut in and out of the harbors with a will more fierce than the wind's. Look high up on the deck above the birds that fly around the hull, and higher still into the rigging over the bridge; nothing but a flag is bending to the wind. If you have binoculars, look again at the flag: Four colored rectangles with the blue and red stars? Or is it the other one, with one star on red and white stripes? Panama and Liberia, respectively. With crews from anywhere in the world— but here.

It's expensive running a ship! What owner is going to put out all that extra money just to have a ship built in American shipyards, to keep up with safety regulations, Coast Guard regulations, and inflated American wages? Eighty percent of American-owned ships are operated under "runaway" flags. U.S. flagships carry less than 5 percent of U.S. trade.

Bog Greg is a tankerman AB (able-bodied seaman). "Remember that tanker that caused all that oil damage a few years back off the Georges' Bank?" he asked me. "That damn ship hadn't been in the shipyard for years. It was sinking long before it sank: the loran [*long-range navigation*] didn't work; the radar didn't work;

they had some guy with a wipers endorsement [lowest rank in the engine room] on the wheel when it stacked up. On top of that, they were forty miles off of where they thought they were. That kind of thing doesn't happen on a U.S. ship.

"The only thing that keeps some American ships under her own flag is the Jones Act. The Jones Act says no foreign ships can take cargo in one U.S. port, then go to another U.S. port without first stopping at a foreign port. It reserves intercoastal shipping to our own. Now they got an act before Congress that would make exceptions to the Jones Act. Most of the other major maritime nations have cargo preference acts that require a certain percentage of their trade sail under their own flag.

"I had to laugh the other night, though. I was bunkering a ship called the *Atlantic Wing* owned by Honda Motor Company, bringing a load of Hondas into Richmond. I looked up at the bridge, and there's the Panamanian flag."

Bill Henerberry is an AB who's been sailing since he was eighteen. "My father was a merchant seaman. I didn't ever see him but once every six months. But whenever I did, he brought me stories from around the world.

"When I first started, I didn't like it much, too regimented. So I spent some time in land jobs, then I really understood regimentation and saw that the sea was a better choice.

"I got to enjoy the sea time, especially after you've been on the beach awhile; it's refreshing. But then you want some adventure, too. We'd pull into a foreign port, and I was an explorer. I'm a class-one tourist of the world; the only place I haven't been is southern Africa. We'd have two or three days in port, enough time to get a feel for a place and talk to the people. There's all kinds of approaches; you can get off the boat and just start walking, or you can pick up a guide and transportation at the docks. Then, it would be back to the ship for some hard work—taking care of the winches, the booms, repairing the rigging, and watching the course till you hit the next port. It was different every day."

This winter, Bill's on standby wages from the Sailor's Union of the Pacific so he can work on the election committee. He spends his days upstairs in the committee room behind the portholed door, forging out amendments from a sea of rugged language.

They broke for lunch, and I asked him if it was still exciting going to sea.

"Ain't been no fun for a long time. It used to be you didn't make any money but you could have a few laughs here and there. Now, there's no time in port and a major problem dealing with boredom in between. Unending monotony for long stretches watching the noon report getting posted on the bulletin board of the mess hall, unremitting boredom followed by maybe the possibility of getting ashore for three to five hours and then go back out there and do it again.

"It used to be like working on an old farm. An animal gets out and you fix the fence; a well runs dry and you dig another one. There was always something different to do. Now the Old Man says, 'Clean up that little area over there.' The shipowner doesn't want any work done at sea.

"The union has been successful in taking the sting out of the pockets, but it hasn't addressed itself to the larger issues of the workplace. That would be a joke if you brought up an issue like that at the negotiating table; we can't even discuss hazards of working with chemical cargo. They'd laugh and say, 'Do you want the work or don't you want the work? You prima donnas are afraid of breathing those fumes? Fine! We'll put coolies in the tank to clean it.' "

So why are you putting all this energy into something that's no longer fun?

"Me and my committee are the temporary stewards of a hundred years of seagoing tradition, and we're taking care in the hope that the future will get better.

"The history of the Sailor's Union of the Pacific is the history of maritime organizing in this country. This is where it all started; it's pivotal. And the reason is because on the west coast we had strong intercoastal trade and immigrants from Scandinavia who took steady jobs on these coasting lumber schooners. They worked the cargo, sailed the ships, and ate right there with the Old Man. What was unusual about that was that most of the time, in the old days, you'd stuff a bunch of degenerates onto a ship and shove them out the Golden Gate and never expect to see them again.

"The Scandinavians were together enough to form the nucleus of the Coast Seamen's Union, which is the predecessor of the Sailor's Union of the Pacific. And out of this, for a great number of years, came nothing but grief, misery, and more grief—and not a little blood.

"Finally they were able to get the Seaman's Act of 1915, which essentially changed us from slaves to workers, because before, if we left the job, even if the ship was in port, we could be proceeded against in criminal court. The Seamen's Act of 1915 was a landmark for sailors. Now we could do business.

"The Unions also play a big part in defining how the officers treat the men, in drawing that line. The captain's word is still law aboard ship, but the crew has redress in court. The crew isn't subject to be lined up and beaten, and that went on right up until lately. If an officer punches you now, you'd better not punch him back, I'll grant you that, but you can haul his ass in court when you get him on the beach. And if the captain gets into a legal beef, the company's going to think about getting rid of him. The company says, 'We don't want trouble. We want our cargo delivered!'

"But, see, the captain's role is completely changed too. He has less and less ability to make decisions about the ship. Now, the agent gets on the telephone and talks to the captain in Hong Kong and tells him what to do next about every little situation. The cargo's all loaded by a computer program portside, and there's a timetable published a month ahead of time telling him when he's coming and going. The captain doesn't say, 'Well, we're not going to sail today' unless he's got a very, very strong reason, and even then, he's putting his job on the line. These ships today are run from the office.

"I was on a tanker a couple of years ago coming from Honolulu to the mainland. The loran broke down, and the officers had to break out the sextant. They hadn't done it in so long that, after they got the rust off it, they sat around for a long time and nervously discussed it. 'Jeez, do we still know how to do this? Does anybody remember; does this thing really work?' I never saw a group of guys so relieved as when they hit that pilot station within a couple of miles. A couple more years, and I wonder if anyone will even know what a sextant's for."

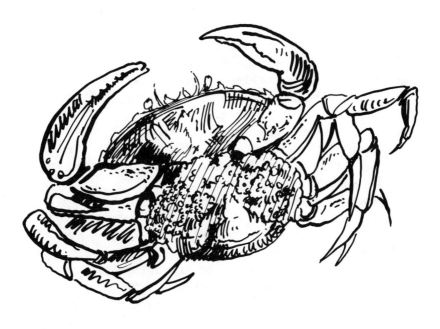

Chapter 14

One Egg in a Million

Having lived with and studied land animals for so many hundreds of years, we've made a lot of assumptions about all animals. It's only in the last few decades of looking into the sea that we're beginning to realize that when it comes to marine animals, we've made almost as many mistakes as we have assumptions. The reproduction of fishes, for example.

Look in the nest of almost any species of bird in the world and it would be a rarity to encounter more than five eggs in the brood; a mammal that gives birth to more than ten young in a single litter is good for a photo in the newspaper; and even the lowly insects, though devoid of maternal investment, number their eggs in the hundreds. But for a fish in the sea to lay a million, or even five million, eggs in a spawn doesn't upset the norm at all. When you consider that the perpetuation of any species requires that only a handful of the progeny survive to adulthood, the fecundity of fishes alone suggests that life in the sea is a very different ball game from what we know on land.

The English sole is a familiar sight on the American dinner plate, even to inlanders from here to the Midwest. For this reason, I decided to use the life cycle of this well-known animal to illustrate the standard of living at sea. And as I scoured the oceanographic libraries and consulted the experts, there emerged the most interesting phenomenon of all: you probably know a lot more about the life cycle of the squirrel in your backyard than the experts know about any fish in the sea.

The English sole is a bottom dweller living in the sand or mud of the midcontinental shelf of our coast (20–80 fathoms of water). The female lays between 150,000 and 2,000,000 eggs, depending on her size. This is known from egg counts made on samples of fish taken from the catches of drag boats. But whether a school of fish all spawn at a given time or whether they stagger their spawn —"We don't know." Does the female dig a red (fish nest)? "We don't think so, but then nobody has ever observed their spawning behavior. We do assume they spawn on the bottom, but that hasn't been proven either."

The next thing that is known for certain about the life cycle of the English sole is that the eggs rise to the surface. In a matter of days, the nutrition of the egg sack is consumed, and the sole hatches into a larval form. This three-millimeter larva, like the larvae of many ocean animals, bears no resemblance to the adult, in morphology, coloration, feeding habits, or behavior. Also like the larvae of many other sea creatures, it has barely enough mobility to move around and catch its own food—it is at the mercy of the winds and currents. If the brood gets carried too far offshore, it will be outside the narrow range of coastal upwelling and will starve to death. If they drift too far south, they will starve for the same reason. Even if they find themselves right in the heart of the upwelling regions, it doesn't mean there's going to *be* upwelling. A week without winds, or with winds coming from the wrong direction, and the whole system collapses. In addition, contrary to previous speculation, it has recently been observed that the English sole larva is a specific plankton feeder; that is, there is only one type of plankton on which it can survive. And with blooms of various types of plankton exploding and collapsing unpredictably over the ocean terrain, and themselves moving and drifting on the winds of chance, you can see that the fate of English sole spawn is a crapshoot every time. One of the more interesting consequences of this uncertainty is that, though a whole generation can be wiped out by an ill wind, by the same token, there are jackpot years when zillions survive. It is the norm among marine animals, especially those inhabiting upwelling regions, that their populations swing through wild fluctuations in density from year to year.

The larva of the English sole drifts around the ocean for eight to ten weeks before it begins to metamorphose into the adult form. During this transition, it drops to the bottom and begins its life as an adult, migrating around in the mud in search of the invertebrates on which it feeds. As the mobile hunter it is as an adult, the life of the English sole is greatly stabilized in relation to its larval days. But still, it is a creature of the broiling and unpredictable sea. The invertebrates of the ocean bottom experience the same wild swings of population as the sole, and so too the predators. And each in the moment is responding to a different roll of dice — one to the density of brown plankton, another to the level of dissolved oxygen, and another to a change of temperature — so that the animals of the fluid sea are at once in different stages of feast and famine and frenzies and deaths en masse to a degree of magnitude that is never experienced on land.

The life cycle of the English sole is actually quite simple compared to many marine animals. Some shrimp, for example, go through as many as twelve larval forms, each stage requiring distinctly different environmental and nutritional conditions. This tendency to pass through multiple larval forms before reaching adulthood is another characteristic of marine animals that is in stark contrast to the development of land animals, whose young tend to eat like, behave like, and look like the adult in everything but size.

Why this is so has recently become the subject of much conjecture. Dan Wickham, a biologist at the Bodega Bay Marine Station, put his views succinctly, "The main thing you have to keep in mind when comparing life in the sea to life on land is that life originated in the sea. The land is much more hostile to life than is the ocean. In fact, the number of species inhabiting the land is minuscule compared with the number of marine species. The vast majority of life on earth is still to be found in the sea. The minute an animal or plant comes onto the land it has to protect itself from drying out, which is the worst possible thing that can happen to any animal. Land creatures have to go to great expense to maintain an ocean environment within; that's a direct consequence of having evolved from the sea. Once on land they don't have the freedom of producing vast quantities of offspring, because each individual offspring has to be invested with an impermeable shell full of nutritious fluids, or it has to be protected in a womb. They still go through as many larval stages as do the animals of the sea, but they do so within the confines of the shell or the womb. At sea, the whole ocean environment is the womb."

The growing interest in the distinctions between life on the land and life in the sea derives from much more than idle curiosity. Two major ocean industries of California in the last two decades have been squared off against the difficulties resulting from these unanticipated differences. The fishing industry, in attempting to manage the stocks, established a system of quotas or maximum sustainable yields for each commercially important species, a system obviously borrowed from our experience with the animals of the land. But it doesn't work in the sea. Not only are the initial population counts extremely expensive and at this point inaccurate, but also, because of the wide swings in population sizes that are characteristic of ocean species, the numbers become meaningless from one year to the next. The emerging aquaculture industry, during the 1960s, was envisioned as the great new hope for a starving world. Countries and industries made initial euphoric investments in its development as if their fortunes were only a year away. Today, for the most part, the money is still flowing in only one direction, as the scientists continue their painstaking attempts to unravel the most basic of questions about the life cycle of the mysterious creatures of the sea.

Chapter 15

A Different Drummer

Of all the extremes of adaptation to the ocean's awful toll on the young, none is more mythic in proportion than the salmon's mighty journey to the mountain streams: a journey that brings life to meet death at a point on a perfect circle, a return through miles of narrowing waters to the exact gravel-bedded streamlet of its birth. A journey to spawning and death, so clear in its resemblance to the migrations of the sperm to the egg as to entwine their meanings in a single reflection.

In a stream so shallow that its full body is no longer submerged in the water, the salmon twists on its side to get a better grip with its tail. Its gillplate torn, big hunks of skin hanging off its side from collisions with a rock, deep gouges in its body, and all around for miles to go there is only the cruelty of more jagged rocks and less and less water to sustain the swim. Surely the animal is dying! And then the salmon leaps like an arrow shot from a bow; some urge and will and passion ignores the animal body and focuses on the stream.

On every continent of the northern hemisphere, from the temperate to the arctic zone, there is hardly a river that hasn't teemed with the salmon's spawn. The Thames, the Rhine, the rivers of France and Spain, Kamchatka and Siberia, Japan (which alone has over two hundred salmon rivers), and the arctic streams of Greenland. From the Aleutians to Monterey Bay, through the broadest byways to the most rugged and narrow gorge, the salmon have made their way home. There are many journeys for which the salmon endure for over a thousand miles. As soon as the ice melts on the Yukon, the king salmon enter the river's mouth, and for a month, the fish swim against the current, fifty miles a day for a total of fifteen hundred miles. And like every other salmon on its run, they fast completely along the way. In other rivers, they scale vertical rocks up to sixty feet high, against turbulent waterfalls hurtling from above. The salmon gets to spawn once in life, and maybe that's reason enough. But this occasion of the salmon's return to the place of its birth is an instinct so unmodifiable and of such purity as to have inspired hundreds of spiritual rites in as many races of human beings.

The salmon arrives battered and starved, with a mate chosen along the way, and never has passion seemed less likely from two more wretched-looking beings. But, there in the gravel of the streamlet, the female fans out a nest with the sweep of her powerful tail and the male fends off intruders. The nest done, the two fish lie next to each other suspended in the water over the nest; their bodies quiver with intense vibrations, and simultaneously they throw the eggs and the sperm. Compared to the millions of eggs thrown by a cod in the stream, the salmon need throw only two to five thousand. Despite the predators and other hazards of the stream, these cold mountain waters are a sanctuary compared to the sea. For the next two or three days, the pair continue nesting and spawning until all the eggs are laid. Then the salmon, whose journey has spanned the ocean and the stream, lies by the nest and dies.

Soon the banks of the streams are stacked with ragged carcasses, and the animals of the woods come down for a feast. The stream lies quiet in the winter's deepening cold. But within a month two black eyes appear through the skin of the eggs. And two weeks later, the water is again alive with the pulsing of millions of small fish feeling the first clumsy kicks of their tails. The fingerlings stay for a while, growing on the insects and larvae that have been nurtured by the forest. Then, one day, they realize what that tail is for and begin their descent to the sea, a journey mapped in their genes by the parents they left behind.

The young salmon arrive in the estuary facing the sea, where they linger again and learn to feed on shrimp, small crustaceans, and other creatures of the brine. Here, also, their bodies complete an upheaval of internal and external changes that allow them to move on to the saltier sea. These adaptations require such extraordinary body transformations that when the same events occur on the stage of evolution they take millions and millions of years. In the life of the salmon, the changes take place in only a matter of months. One of life's most prohibitive barriers—that between fresh and salt water—is crossed, and the salmon swim back and forth, in and out of the sea, trying it on for size. Then one day, the youngsters do not return. The stream is only a distant memory drifting further and further back in the wake of time, only different —a memory that will resurrect and demand that its path be retraced.

So accessible is the salmon's life in the stream that more is known about the reproduction of this fish than any other ocean animal. With the ease of placing cameras underwater, there isn't any aspect of this dramatic cycle that hasn't been captured in full color in some of the most spectacular film footage ever made. But once the salmon enters the sea, the story of its life is a secret as deep and dark as the farthest reaches of the ocean it roams. Not the human eye, nor its most sophisticated aids, from satellite to sonar, has ever caught more than a glance of the salmon at sea. Extensive tagging programs have been carried out, but they tell us little more than that the salmon is likely to be found anywhere within thousands of miles of its origins, and even this is only a sliver of the picture because the tags are recovered only when the salmon is caught by fishermen, and they work solely within the narrow coastal zone. Along with a few other pelagic fishes, like the tuna, that claim vast stretches of sea for their pasture, the salmon's life remains one of the most mysterious on earth.

In the eight years that I fished the salmon along the California coast, I only once saw a salmon that wasn't on the end of a hook. It was on a sunny afternoon anchored in the lee of Point Arena Cove, a rare afternoon because the usually murky waters were clear as a crystal. Even the rocks and plants thirty-five feet below were as visible as the floor of an aquarium. I was supposed to be repairing some tangled gear, but my eyes were fixed on a school of anchovies suspended in the water about ten feet under my stern. We always referred to these schools as bait balls, but I never could have imagined the perfection in the precision and flow of their formations. It was like a perfectly ordered fluid galaxy. Each fish of the thousands is always perfectly aligned and equidistant from the fish next to it while the whole school revolves, turns, and changes its shape from one form to another without ever losing its roundness. I was completely entranced by this weightless and beautiful dance when it suddenly exploded into a thousand parts and in as many directions. All I saw was a broad swath of silver rippling through the school like a bullet, stunning and crippling any fish within the shock of its path. Three times, before I could even blink, the salmon was back through the same path, swallowing everything that couldn't move with the speed of light—an attacker that made the big cats of the Serengeti seem delicate in their pursuit of just one animal of the flock at a time. And yet most of the time the salmon's belly is filled with shrimp or copepods (minute crustaceans), the staple foods of a simple ocean grazer.

Knowing everything I could about salmon was my only path to a paycheck, but it took me a very long time to realize that I would never know anything for sure. You make the mistake of drawing a conclusion and the animal will prove you wrong within the day. The salmon swims with the current, it swims against the current; it shuns clear water, it goes wild in the light; it swims alone, it swims in tight schools; it feeds every morning at dawn, it doesn't feed for a week; it mills for a month outside the mouth before going upstream, it goes up overnight. And the salmon's erratic habits are no more confounding than its wide swings of mood. Wild, sassy, babyish, lazy, mean, cold, hot, skittish, bold, flippy, docile—you put your lines in the water in the morning and from one hour to the next you never know which animal you're going to be dealing with. What strange spirit wraps these moods like a wild vine around the salmon's iron core of majesty and will? What wild uncharted journeys are logged by the fish at sea? What yearning shuns the freedom and sends them back to the stream? Of all the fish in the sea, why is it the salmon that gets into your dreams, and into the festivities and totems and religions of peoples around the world? For all agree, the salmon is the noblest fish of them all.

If you want your kids to see more than the broken spirits of the animals of the zoo, here's a list of places where you can stand on the banks of the stream and watch the salmon return from the sea. For more detailed information call the office of Fish and Game located nearest your home (see Marine Directory).

River	Closest Town	Season
Feather River	Oroville	fall and spring run
Klamath River	Yreka	October run
Trinity River	Lewiston	Sept./Oct. run
Russian River	Healdsburg	Sept./Oct. run
American River	Folsom	fall run

Chapter 16

River Be Damned

Evaporated ocean air, say the experts, hits the mountains and falls as snow. The snow melts and follows gravity back to the sea in the rivers. Rivers, supposedly, are merely the gorged conduits for the latter part of this process, the line from here to there on the hydrographic flow charts. A loss of potential energy, said the power companies. Any drop of water that goes back into the oceans is a wasted drop of water, said the California farmers. So we built the dams, installed the valves, reaped the energy, watered the crops, and only then did we understand that rivers are much, much more.

Certainly you've heard about the plight of the salmon. For

years now the salmon's been carrying the ball for the river in the interminable battles over dams and diversions. The reason is obvious and worth a moment of review. Consider, for example, the Red Bluff Diversion Dam (also known as the fish-killer dam), built in the early 1960s to divert upper Sacramento River water through the Tehama-Colusa Canal down to the agricultural lands of the south. Plates were built to keep the fish from getting diverted, but the fish get caught in the plates; a ladder was built for the fish, but it was built in the wrong place (if they had put it in the right place, they wouldn't be able to count the fish). The swirling waters and backwash around the dam are extremely disorienting to the salmon's delicate homing mechanisms. They get confused and make wrong turns. Because the fish are so much less alert around the dams, a predator has bloomed in the disaster. Squawfish hang at the base of the dam in great numbers, gobbling up the young salmon, getting fat, and multiplying. And the lighting on the dam increases nocturnal predation. Gravel beds are needed for the fish to spawn. Not only have these beds been buried in the lakes formed behind the dam, but the few remaining spawning grounds to the south are losing all their gravel to the wash of the river; this is natural, but it's also natural that the gravel be replaced by more gravel coming down from the streams, another process blocked by the dams. In 1950, there were four hundred thousand salmon running up this section of the river; today there are only a hundred thousand. Or, looking at the larger picture, 96 percent of the original spawning grounds in the Sacramento River system are destroyed; many stocks of salmon are extinct—which shouldn't come as any more of a shock than the fact that running over a watch with a steamroller stops its ticking.

The value of the upper Sacramento salmon, according to a duly consecrated computation, is $80 million a year. That's about the bare minimum entrance fee for participation in the great California water debate. Without the salmon, the river wouldn't even have a voice. But the fact is, there are thousands of processes and organisms in the river that have been disrupted and destroyed. The sea perch is nearly extinct; the marshes on the flyways of migrating birds have shriveled; and we see in San Francisco Bay, the bloom of the estuaries is stagnating because of the river's diversion. Still, these are only spin-off effects of disrupting the larger life of the river. And though the river itself has never been given a monetary value, it's only because its value is as immeasurable as the price of the dawn; and though its life has rarely been chronicled, it is functioning, nonetheless, as a vital organ in the body of nature, a great membranous capillary between the land and the sea that is the wellspring of all the rest. As breathing is the consummate vital sign of an animal's life, so for the river is meandering.

Tom Kraemer grew up in Orland, California, hunting and fishing along the Sacramento River with his father. "When I was ten," he says, "my father took me down to a spot where we'd been many times before, and when we walked in, the woods that I thought were there forever were gone. They'd brought the bulldozers in to make farmland, and I couldn't believe it. I said to my father, 'Why'd they do that?' and I guess for the lack of something better to say, he said, 'Well, that's progress.' And I decided at that point that I couldn't ever accept that as progress. I suppose I've been beating my head against it ever since."

For a number of years Tom did his own meandering. He went to Chico State and got his degree in agriculture and then worked for a few years in fruit packing plants. Then he went to Saudi Arabia to help start wheat fields in the desert, came back and taught for a while, and then decided to go for his master's degree. When it came time to do his thesis, he thought, "Well, I'm going to do something on the river. I'm down there all the time and I know it like the back of my hand." His thesis, completed in 1981, is a pioneering description of the river's way of life.

If you travel along the path of the Sacramento, something you will notice, even if you never set foot outside your car, is that the river takes up only a small portion of its bed. What you are seeing is evidence of the river's meandering. From one year to the next, the river's path can vary over a hundred feet. Where the river might go in the next hundred or two hundred years can be determined by looking on a geological map at the area's distribution of Columbian soils. This is where the river has been meandering over the last million years. It is in this process that the land and the river are replenished by each other.

Here is a description of one aspect of that process as described in Tom's thesis. It is called dry succession. Erosion occurs naturally and continually on the outside bends in the river. On the other side of the river, opposite the eroding face, is the point bar, where deposition is taking place. During the generally stable time of the river, mid-May through mid-July, the point bar is seeded with willow and cottonwood. The result is a band of young tree growth at the water's edge. Flooding in the following winter deposits additional sediment, since the new band of growth slows the current as it flows through the vegetation. At the same time, erosion is continuing on the outer edge. With each movement of the river, another band of trees is started, more soil is deposited, and the effect is a gradient forest in which the taller and older trees are set back from the river. At the same time, the loop of the river is becoming exaggerated, until the shape of its course can be described as an oxbow loop. There are such places on the river where you can travel three or four miles by water and cover an overland distance of only one mile. The loops finally become so extreme that the river cuts itself a new path along the shortest distance between the two points. The meander loop is abandoned and becomes what's called the oxbow lake. The oxbow lake slowly clogs with alluvium and sediment, but for a long time remains a rich habitat for fish. The newly straightened section of river soon develops a subtle new curve and restarts the process in one direction or the other, meandering, as it has done for a million years.

The band of vegetation and forest that follows in the river's swath is also one of the river's main sources of energy. The leaves and sticks fall into the water and decay, giving rise to the detritus that feeds the river's herbivores. The dense riparian forest feeds droves of insects, which fall in the river and feed the fish. The fish live and die, their bodies mixing with the sediment that gets trapped by the forest during the floods; or the bear eats the fish and defecates in the woods. And this is not to mention the birds, frogs, and marshy plants that are all part of this intricate capillary between the land and the sea. As the forest ages, its banks are again eroded by the meandering of the river. It's what the Indians call the roundness of things.

A second focus of Tom's thesis was to look at this and other processes of the river as they have been affected by man. The alluvial soils of the river respond in miracles to the farmer's touch, and the farmers want to go right up to the river's edge. The dense vegetation is cut, and the farmers reap crop yields that can be equaled in few places in the world. The river swells and runs rampant as it has always done, only now its shoreside currents are unchecked by the baffling of vegetation. And the farmland is swept away. The farmer runs to the government and says, You've got to do something, and the Corps of Engineers puts in rock walls (riprap) at a cost of two hundred dollars a foot, which in the total program adds up to millions of dollars. And the riprap buys the farmer another three or four years.

But the river keeps meandering. Tom has lots of photos of washed-out riprap and abandoned riprap sitting in the oxbow lakes; yet the farmers keep calling for more. Now the Board of Reclamation has come up with the 1983 Manning Plan, which is supported by the Corps of Engineers. The plan, the ultimate coup on the river, is to riprap every bend. As one engineer put it, "We're going to freeze the river in place."

Tom proposes a nonstructural alternative: instead of spending the $200 million on riprap that obviously doesn't work, the state should use the money to buy river lands as they come up for sale and create a riparian corridor, a meander zone. This land can be leased out to be farmed or it can be maintained wild. But when the river comes in, that's the end of the lease. The soil eroded from one place will be deposited in another, as it always has been. The river will stay healthy, and the benefits, says Tom, are forever. "But the Corps of Engineers isn't interested. They want to put rocks on the banks. That's engineers' work."

The $200 million, of course, is a trickle compared to the cost of dams and diversion; the riprap is just a little hardening of the artery compared to the major hemorrhaging going on upstream as waters are diverted south. Arguing for bugs and cottonwoods would put the committees to sleep. But the bugs and trees and microbes are the salmon and the soil and sediment and the meander of the river, all inextricably entwined, and all in a moment of time.

The oneness, the roundness of things, is something we give lip service to now and then. But our own lives and institutions are themselves too fragmented and compartmentalized to allow this understanding to be put to practice. What comes much more naturally as a solution to these problems is the widely used philosophy of mitigation. You let us build the dam, and we'll build you a hatchery. You let us build the bridge, and we'll put aside some marshland for posterity. Mitigation has become the great successful compromise for developers and environmentalists alike because it's the kind of deal that falls right in front of the blind spot in our way of life. But mitigation will not work, any more than tuning up three cylinders of an engine and smashing the fourth. What good is a healthy lung if the other is full of cancer? It's the roundness of things that has to be preserved, not the salmon that swims in its sphere.

Chapter 17

Ray Welsh

And then there are the guys who merely push the starter button, kick it in gear, and dead reckon a course full ahead between the devil and the deep blue sea, as certain of the good as if it were an unbroken line on a trusted old chart. For half of his life Ray Welsh managed a box-making crew in Sacramento; for the second half of his life he fished, and on the side, as patiently and quietly as you would whittle a stick on a summer afternoon, Ray carved out a future for salmon in California.

I didn't really know Ray when I was fishing; I remember a few times when he'd stand up for a couple of minutes at the end of a salmon trollers meeting, and without philosophy or fanfare he'd ask if we'd bring our old trolling wire up to his house so he could keep the birds out of the rearing ponds, or he'd ask if we could throw a salmon off to the side of our next load to help pay for another batch of feed. It certainly didn't sound like the stuff of revolution, but then again, it's funny how a subtle thing like that can leave a very deep impression. Ten years later as I began work on this book, Ray was the first guy I called on when I went to Fort Bragg.

"What were you doing, Ray, with that old trolling wire and the fish we put off to the side?"

"Well, in 1948, I saw we were in trouble with the salmon."

"1948?" I said, surprised anybody even thought about those things back then, but Ray just continued on.

"You see, the catch kept going down. There were fewer fish and less spawning area, and something had to be done."

What Ray did in the next thirty-five years was organize the diverse interests along the coast, convince the Department of Fish and Game of the need for stronger hatchery programs, develop new techniques, and personally put over two million salmon back in the sea. He brought together sportsmen, commercial fishermen, the lumber companies, hatchery biologists, and state representatives into a group called Salmon Unlimited that today functions as the main salmon protective group in the state. The remarkable thing is that Ray did this in 1950, back in the days when most of these groups hated each other so much they wouldn't even get in the same room together.

"In any mass of people," says Ray, "you'll get four or five who'll put their shoulder to the wheel, then you'll get the guys who'll downgrade you, but most of the guys are just skeptical and it just takes a little while to convince them.

"The first thing I did was organize the Silver Salmon Committee in Fort Bragg. In the very beginning, we were just three or four guys who waited for just the right time. Then one day, we each went out and told a couple more guys that we needed some help down at Pudding Creek, moving some logs. We didn't tell them much more than that. We got some chain saws, borrowed a big Caterpillar and some big cables, set it all up by a big logjam in the creek, built a big fire off in one spot, and waited. About twenty-five guys showed up, and we went to work.

"It was winter, and we were up to our necks in the water, cutting logs and pulling 'em out. Then we'd take a couple of minutes to get warm by the fire and go back to work. That logjam was over two hundred feet long and twelve feet high, and we cleared it in one day. And when we cut the last logs free, the salmon that were trapped in the river just downstream swam right through and on up the river to spawn. I think we convinced quite a few people that day. If you want to organize something, you have to show that you're willing and capable to work—otherwise, forget it."

The next thing Ray did was to get the lumber companies and the fishermen talking to each other—no mean feat since the hatred between these two groups had solidified over the years. Along the full length of the coast up to Washington, they share the same towns in about the same way two hungry cats share a piece of meat.

"I used to have big banquets," said Ray, "and invite everyone —Fish and Game, lumber company officials, lumbermen, town officials, fishermen—everybody. You know, food can heal a lot of wounds. At first, the lumbermen would come tongue in cheek and a chip on their shoulder. But they've changed day and night since then, even though there's a lot left to be done."

These banquets started by Ray thirty years ago continue today as the Annual July Fourth Fort Bragg Salmon Barbecue, an event that draws people from all over the state to celebrate the sweet taste of salmon, the fishing exhibits, and the Fort Bragg summer. Last year over four thousand people came to the barbecue. And as no small aside, it raised thirty-five thousand dollars to support the salmon-raising projects of the Fort Bragg Fishermen's Marketing Association, another group started by Ray.

But there can be no doubt, Ray's proudest accomplishment is those fish swimming about in his ponds. Right now, he has a hundred thousand kings at Ten Mile Creek and two hundred thousand kings in Hollow Tree Creek ready to be released at the first rain.

"We've made a lot of mistakes, but you have to learn from your experience. I used to think the big hatcheries were the answer, but not any more. You know, the salmon isn't a dumb fish, it's a majestic fish. It has a lot of dignity, and you have to take that into consideration. I think they must pick their partners in the ocean before they start up the stream. I saw a big sixty-pound female once who picked a five-pound male as her mate, and he fought like anything to protect her. But I know at Pudding Creek when we'd trap them and separate them we'd upset that relationship a bit. Another thing we learned was when we'd take a stream and clear out every log and twig, and then watch in amazement because the fish wouldn't stop there and spawn. Then the next year, we put big boulders in the stream and that made currents and activity in the water and the fish were as happy as clams. The big thing, though, is that you gotta have a guy round the clock at the pond. Not just any guy, it's gotta be a guy that thinks like a fish and has genuine concern for the fish, 'cause you have to wet-nurse them all the time. If one fish out of two hundred thousand gets sick, you better know about it, fish him out, and figure out what's wrong, because there's no better carrier of infection than water. You have to pay attention to these fish like you raise a child; but you know, the reward is just as great.

'The one thing that's been a disappointment to me is the hope I used to have that we could get these streams to be self-perpetuating, but now I have a question in my mind if it will ever be that way again. We've put too much silt in the rivers, particularly in the gravel areas. I don't think we'll ever get it flushed out the way nature used to have it. It will improve, but once you mess up nature, I don't know if you can ever curl her hair exactly like it was before."

Chapter 18

Ten Mile Creek Pond

"Drive north of Fort Bragg about fifteen minutes, you'll see the big sign that says Georgia Pacific, take a right and go up the lumber road that follows the stream, through the gravel pit, and you'll run right into the trailer sitting by the pond," says Ray Welsh. "Don will be there, he never leaves the fish except to buy groceries."

Right off the highway, the logging road joins the river in a beautiful grassy valley full of yellow flowers wafting in the summer breeze. I promise myself I'm going to move up here and stay forever, in the midst of the colors and smells of the northland. The river just lies there in the grass, like a lazy old cat taking up the heat of the sun. Only the barely perceptible twirl of a leaf on its skin says the river continues to breathe, deep in its sleep, waiting for the rains of fall. Oh, yes, I remember now, northern California in the winter, when the rivers turn to rogues. And this little wooden bridge? Quiet as a picture on a wall, I bet they've rebuilt the thing as often as June follows spring.

Around the bend the hills turn into mountains and crowd in on the stream, and the sunlight stays trapped in the trees. Salmon country, where the water runs cold through the dark forest floor. And sure enough, there's the trailer and Don, carrying a sack of feed on his back.

"Don Bradley? The last time I saw you was on the fishing grounds off Shelter Cove. Ray didn't tell me it was you. What are you doing up here?"

"I'm taking these sacks of feed down to that locked container. You see that shed on the hill? The bears ripped it apart, ripped open the sacks of feed, ate themselves sick, and got diarrhea all over the place. That was enough for me. You see how I built that box? That bear can come down here all he wants now."

"Is Audrey here too, and Joe? Aren't you fishing anymore?"

"We've still got the boat, but we tied it up for the summer to do this. Audrey's in the trailer, and Joe's running around here somewhere. There's plenty of work here for all of us. We've got two hundred thousand fish right there that we raised from babies, and every day they have to be fed twice, and we have to measure the oxygen, the temperature, and do a bunch of other tests on the water. We got to watch all the fish so close we know them all by name. And just taking care of the gates and keeping the gravel boundaries in place can be an all-day job by itself. You see how the pond's dug out? So the natural stream water flows through? These fish are getting a lot of natural food too, not like in the cement ponds. We get a much better growth rate this way, and when we let them go, they can already fend for themselves. One thing we don't do, though, is tag the fish, because that stresses them too much."

"What's here for Joe to do? He had such an important job on the boat, sitting all day up in the bow when it was foggy and barking every time you came near another boat. He must feel kind of downgraded out here."

"No, Joe's got work here too. He gets up in the middle of the night and chases away predators—like the otters, they're the worst. They wouldn't leave ten fish in this pond if Joe didn't chase them away."

"Right," says Audrey, "and look what he did with the bear, he hid under the bunk till it was gone."

The little four-inch fish were flipping like silver coins on the surface of the pond, catching the dimming light of day on their scales. Joe was barking, and it was getting close to time to feed.

"These fish are getting antsy, they want to go downstream. Pretty soon we'll have to open the gates and let them free. It'll take them a couple of weeks to get down to the estuary. They'll mill around down there for a while, and all of a sudden Mother Nature will say go, and off they'll go to the sea. Our big hope here is that this is one of the places we can start a natural run like there was thirty years ago; we want to take hatchery fish and make them go wild. But a funny thing. You know where these eggs come from? We had to get the eggs from Wisconsin, from the salmon they brought there from the West Coast twenty years ago. And the reason we had to go to Wisconsin is that all the Sacramento fish have the virus, and you don't know when it's going to break out. And all the Klamath and Trinity fish have another disease called IHN. These fish haven't been to the ocean for twenty years, and look at them, they're raring to go."

"One more thing I wanted to ask you, Don. Is this lumber company property we're on?"

"That's right, we couldn't exist without the lumber companies. They gave us the space and the equipment for digging it out."

"Sure," I said. "They're the ones that killed the runs in the first place."

"You know, sometimes you have to let bygones be bygones. In 1979 a group came to us from Masonite, Louisiana Pacific, Georgia Pacific, and Harwoods, and they said, 'What can we do for you?' And we said, 'Well, what do you want us to do for you?' And they said, 'Nothing. You guys are having a hard time now, and we're part of the community.' So together, we're giving some fish back to Mother Nature and improving the economic health of the town."

Chapter 19

Hatcheries

Today there are close to fifty different citizen groups in the state involved in one way or another with salmon restoration. There are also nine state hatcheries producing millions of fingerlings every year, and still the fate of the salmon hangs in precarious balance. And some say there isn't a true salmon left in California.

Methods vary from hatchery to hatchery, but typically the salmon are diverted from their upstream run and corralled into the facility. The fish are killed, and their eggs and sperm are squeezed into a bucket where fertilization takes place. Inside, the hatcheries look like the boiler room of a big ship, with valves and pipes running every which way for directing controlled amounts of water throughout the ponds. Along one wall are tiers of metal trays stacked one above the other, each with hundreds of indentations for holding the fertilized eggs. A flow of water is trickled down through the tiers to simulate a running mountain stream. After the eggs have hatched, the fry are placed in a series of cement raceways where the fish are fed and nursed until they reach four to six inches in length, the usual size for release. At the hatcheries that are located near the mouth of a river, the fish are generally released into the river, but at the hatcheries on the Sacramento River system, the smolts are loaded into tanks, anesthetized, and trucked down to the Carquinez Strait for release. The biology of the upper Delta is so distorted from its original status that the young salmon can no longer survive its passage.

From the very beginning these hatcheries have been operating from one crisis to the next, and heading the list are the recurrent outbreaks of baffling diseases. Whenever you crowd any undomesticated animal, from humans down to crustaceans, rapid transmission of an infective agent is a certain consequence, and nothing transmits disease faster than water. Not only are the diseases of hatchery fish explosive, they are also for the most part incurable. Complete wipeouts and "crashes" are a common occurrence.

Water quality is another problem. Siltation and pollution in the streams is one of the factors that necessitated the hatcheries in the first place, but building hatcheries didn't make the problem go away. Salmon require cold, clear, oxygenated running water inside the hatchery or out, and where are you going to get it if not from the stream? One attempted solution to this problem has been to build a couple of high-tech hatcheries with computer monitoring of water conditions and elaborate recirculating systems. The Mad River hatchery in northern California is one of these. One of the fruits of this system has been an even faster spread of disease. In the spring of 1983, 1.8 million young salmon came down with a viral disease that had never been seen before in the state, and it was lethal. But before all the fish were dead, a decision was made to destroy them, all 1.8 million, in hopes that the disease would never be seen again. "The first thing I'd do if I had the money," says one Fish and Game hatchery biologist, "is get a bulldozer and go up there and level that place and the other one like it. They've been nothing but trouble."

Disease and water quality are the kind of visible problems that are at least recognized by everyone involved, even though the remedies are hotly disputed. But there is another, more insidious problem in the hatcheries—one much further reaching in its consequences and one only recently brought to discussion. In 1980, the Brown administration created the California Gene Resources Program with the Department of Food and Agriculture designated as the lead agency. The charge of the group was to identify measures required to safeguard the gene resources of California, a rather ominous-sounding commodity ringing with the macabre overtones of a science fiction novel. Actually the concern arises out of some mundane little disasters like the corn leaf blight of 1970. The problem is that when we breed an organism to make it better, we're talking faster growth, size regularity, resistance to particular diseases, color; in other words, we're talking about convenience and economic value, not about helping the organism. The result, by definition, is elimination of all the genes that produce an organism varying from the norm. Gene diversity doesn't sell well at the supermarket, but the inevitable price is that the hardiness and vigor of the organism are lost. And when unexpected disease or stress comes along, there is no segment of the population left with the genetic strength to resist it. In 1970, 15 percent of the U.S. corn crop contracted the blight, and 15 percent of the crop was wiped out. There have been so many recent disasters of this nature that teams of agricultural scientists are desperately scouting the wilds of foreign countries in hope of finding a "real" plant left somewhere that can be bred back into the plastic mold. The consequences of losing gene diversity in our highly engineered domestic stocks is a dangerous game of Russian roulette, but with animals that have to maintain their ability to survive in the wild, this kind of monkey business is certain disaster.

In 1983, the Gene Resources Program was disbanded, but not before it managed to publish a thought-provoking report called "The Anadromous Salmonid—Genetic Resources." The report states that in general, hatchery fish are genetically inferior to wild fish in many traits affecting their survival. A number of studies have shown that hatchery fish are less wary and less disease-resistant, and exhibit much more straying than a wild fish, which means that a lot of them can't even find their way home. The reasons for this are worth understanding if you wish to continue living in a world with real animals.

Suppose you take only the largest fish for breeding, a common practice in the hatcheries until very recently, the idea being to improve their growth rate. Well, suppose you decided to breed only seven-foot-tall human beings. Obviously, you'd be picking up a disproportionate number of metabolic defects, bone problems, and a host of other weirdnesses. The same goes for a fish. In addition, there is a reason that an animal population fluctuates around a given median size. What would happen to a population of fast-growing fish during one of the ocean's normal lulls in food production? They're going to starve to death, because they're not really salmon, they're hyper-metabolic freaks.

Another whim of bio-alchemy has been to alter (deliberately or inadvertently) the time of the year that the fish return to the hatcheries by breeding only late or early returnees. It's only just beginning to dawn on a very few of those involved that each individual stock of salmon has been adapting to a particular river condition over thousands of years, and the salmon itself has already chosen the best time. This stock concept, the understanding that the fish from different river systems are genetically distinct, has serious implications for a current practice in California hatcheries. To date many millions of salmon eggs have been trucked from one river system to another. These planted hatchery fish exhibit very high rates of straying into neighboring streams. No one knows how many of these wayward fish have passed on their genetic differences and deficiencies to the wild stocks in the state. It's also been a common practice to eliminate diseased fish from the breeding. But think about it — if that sick fish made it from the ocean all the way up the arduous, grueling path of the river and still isn't dead, don't you think that fish has something inside worth passing on to the next generation?

The real dilemma here is that even if you eliminate all methods of conscious selection, the underlying problem of unnatural selection goes on just by virtue of the fish being raised in the hatchery.

One thing the hatcheries always brag about is that they have a lower juvenile mortality rate than in nature. Mortality, however, is Mother Nature doing her job of keeping the species strong. That way there aren't a bunch of weak fish out there eating up the available food, fish that won't make it back to the river to spawn; that way there aren't a bunch of weak fish in the school that will contract every disease that comes along and pass it to the rest of the school—and so on. In the hatchery, the young fish are raised in buckets, trays, and cement raceways; every step of their early life is protected with antibacterial and antifungal agents. Nature is no longer acting to select out the young fish that can't hunt the insects, or the fish that don't know to hide under a rock at the first sign of a predator. They survive in the artificial environment of the hatchery and live to pass on their nonadaptive genes. In the same way, a female, for example, who doesn't have the proper nest-building instinct would loose her entire brood to the mortality of the wild stream; but in the hatchery, which mistakenly boasts of high survival rates, this same female can produce up to five thousand surviving young—all carrying the same defect. It doesn't take long before you've created a breed of fish that is no more suited to the stream than the poodle is to the woods.

What difference does it make, if the fish are coming back to the hatcheries to breed anyway? One immediate problem is that these fish don't always make it back to the hatchery; as the Gene Resources Program report says, they get lost a lot; they go up the wrong stream and then breed with the wild fish. And now many fishermen believe there isn't a real salmon left in the state of California.

Since 90 percent of the spawning grounds are destroyed, we're stuck with hatcheries and breeding management for a long time. But as long as we pursue things like fast growth and low juvenile mortality and call it an improvement on nature, then it's not the salmon we're saving. "They took the beautiful salmon," says one fisherman, "and they made it into just another dumb fish."

Chapter 20

Seabirds

You can travel for days over a sea of such lifeless expanse that your mind begins conjuring images of journeys you've never made—the march of desert nomads on the great Sahara, a lapse into Siberian latitudes where time itself is frozen, the specter of a trillion footprints buried in the snow on their way to the poles. But none of these mental fantasies captures the depth of the desert sea, or the maddening reality that the spot you search for could be suddenly blooming in your wake where you passed only hours before. Neither the compass, nor charts, nor yesterday's news can plot your course to the spontaneous oases at sea. But, there, way out on the far horizon, is a flurry no more perceptible than a wind-rustled bush with miles of dunes in between, and its beckoning is no less resistible.

The bow is locked on the spot, and within a couple of hours you are surrounded by the frenzied screeches and excited flights of the birds, thousands of birds—whale birds, albacore birds, partner birds—all gorging on the feast beneath their wings. How do they know? How do they always find these places? And before you can ponder, the lines pull tight with the fish schooling in the depths, feeding on the bait, on the shrimp, on the plankton that bloomed with the rise of the sun. A fountain of life, hidden, unseen but for the birds that carry its secret aloft.

How is it that if the sky is empty from horizon to horizon and you throw a handful of bait over the stern, the birds are there before the bait has time to sink? Or in the middle of a sunny day when the feed is settled sixty fathoms below and you see hundreds of birds from a dozen different species sitting patiently on the surface waiting for its upward migration, how do they know it's there? Can they hear the bait below?

We know that all seabirds have keen eyes; most of them have powerful wings for long flights; and all of them have intricately engineered feathers to keep the water from robbing their heat. But how, in the vastness and vacancy of ocean terrain, do the birds always find the spot before the fisherman, who has radar, radio, sonar, and even the eyes of the satellites?

There is even less known about seabirds than about fish. There's not a whole lot of politicians pounding the halls of Congress for the necessary grants. Even potential recipients of grants tend to make excuses for the situation: "Well, the seabirds are on top of the food chain, nothing eats them"; "There's no fat on a seabird—wouldn't taste good"; "We don't have a guano industry in California, no boobies here. Did you know that in Peru it used to be death if you killed a guano bird?"

There is a total of four full-time bird observatories in all of North America. The Point Reyes Bird Observatory in northern California is one of them and the only one that spends a significant amount of time on the seabirds of the Pacific. Not surprisingly, its funding is grab-bag; it operates with lots of volunteers and people bearing gifts. They came together in 1965. A handful of biologists who were banding birds in the area began getting contracts as a group, adding to their staff, expanding their area of interest, and in 1968 they had pulled together enough funds to do an intensive study of the nesting colonies on the Farallon Islands.

Quite obviously, they didn't pick the Farallons for its climate. Desolation is all it offers to the human soul, but for over twelve major species of seabird, it is the largest rookery on the west coast. So many birds gather here that at feeding time the rugged eighty-acre rock seems to levitate with the beat of a million wings; the noise, if you close your eyes, becomes the haunting screech of the underworld, and the smell, without a breeze to carry it off, is enough to make you pull anchor. To the north, you have to reach the Queen Charlotte Islands before you come across anything comparable. To the south, the bird life is relatively sparse on the Channel Islands; the water on the back side of the islands is too deep to harbor the necessary bait, and the upwellings in the area are much weaker. San Miguel and San Nicolas have small rookeries of auklets, gulls, and cormorants, and Anacapa Island is the main breeding ground for the brown pelican in California. But the overall numbers just don't match the Farallons.

So every day five or six members of the Point Reyes Bird Observatory huddled behind their blinds, stoics in the wind, and took copious notes, measurements, and photographs on everything from egg mortality to mating fidelity. Thousands of birds were banded, and because of the fortuitous fact that most seabirds nest within fifty yards of their birthplace, as many stories can now be told. One of these, the story of cormorant #45136, is included here.

During the same period, another group from the observatory, in conjunction with the Audubon Society and the Mono Lake Committee, set up shop at Mono Lake in eastern California. All the feeder streams to the lake have been diverted to supply water to Los Angeles, and the lake is changing fast. The water level is dropping, the salinity rising, the eggs of the brine shrimp are experiencing increased mortality, and the California gull, which broods over 95 percent of its population in this unique ecosystem, is unable to feed its young. The Mono Lake group had taken on the rather disheartening task of measuring the rate at which the horse is running away from the barn.

In 1981 almost all the chicks died. Not many brine shrimp had been able to survive the increased salinity, so there wasn't much feed for the young chicks. The main island on which the gulls laid their eggs was now connected to the mainland because of the low-ered water level, and the coyotes had a feast. Some of the gulls moved to the smaller islands to lay their eggs, but the smaller islands had no brush to shade the nests from the heat and the eggs fried.

As you might guess, not many tears were shed over the col-lapse of this brood. Los Angeles certainly had no intention of miti-gating the loss of a flock of air rats, dump dwellers, screechers, or airport pests, as they were variously called.

Dave Shuford, a member of the research project who had gotten his Ph.D. in ornithology, specializing in sea gulls, saw it differently. "They're an opportunistic bird, a very social animal. Sure they're scavengers, and they're one of the few animals that has adapted very well to civilization. They're also very beautiful." The group felt that Los Angeles should be accountable for any living species they threaten to destroy, and currently the seagull is having its day in court.

All seabirds breed on land, and this is the one thing that allows groups like the observatory to fill in our understanding of their reproductive habits. Most of their lives, however, are spent at sea, and what that life is like remains a mystery. Getting *any* kind of grant to study seabirds requires some serious scratching, but get-ting a grant that would provide a boat is as likely as getting a break from the IRS. And how are you going to study a seabird without a boat?

Well, some people won't let such trivia stand in their way. There's a guy who works for the Division of Mines and Geology for the State of California mapping out geological hazards, lique-faction hazards, faults, wind erosion, and volcanic hazards and then taking his findings to high-pressure meetings with state plan-ners. But for two hours every day, Richard Kilbourne found a way to study the lives of birds at sea without spending an extra dime. He took the ferry to and from work in San Francisco, and every day the boat passed through some of the most popular feed-ing grounds for over fifty different species of seabirds—behind Angel Island, behind Alcatraz, in front of the Golden Gate. Mr.

Kilbourne brought his binoculars, and in just a few years he'd amassed a mountain of data.

"Nothing's known about these birds," he says, "because they're inaccessible and they live in harsh weather conditions that nobody can be expected to endure. But the ferryboat is perfect. It gives you a nice glass-enclosed platform for observation, and on days when you don't feel like taking the weather up on deck, you can watch the birds from the bar."

The first thing Mr. Kilbourne did was standardize and run off copies of a data sheet that would allow him to quickly record his observations. Each sheet had a checklist for the fifty seabirds he was likely to see in the area, to enable him to make a daily census of the birds. Some days he encountered over a thousand just on his way to work. The worksheet is also laid out for easy recording of temperature, tide, weather conditions, time, visibility, sea conditions, and so on. And then there is a section for intuitive observations: are the birds feeding, fighting, fidgeting, flying, or whatever.

"The main thing I was trying to do was gather enough data to see patterns over the years, to gain some insight into the tremendous fluctuations that occur in the seabird populations. But at the same time, I ended up making a lot of friends. People always asked me if I was a researcher and I'd tell them, 'Nah, this is just a way not to have too many drinks every time I ride the ferry.' Then I'd explain what I was doing and give them a checklist and get them going on the project, too.

"Do you know about the lady from Ohio? She had a bird feeder outside her window and decided to take a few notes on the birds that came to the feeder. She described what she saw for a year: the color of the eggs, how they made their nests, how many eggs they laid, simple things—and she only did it for a year. And even today, that information remains the classic work on the more than a dozen species she watched. Even less is known about seabirds. Anyone can make a contribution just by taking a notebook and a pair of binoculars down to the beach or out on a pier. It's a great hobby—a sport—and it's exciting for the kids, too. Just don't expect a market for it."

A few months ago, Richard's office was moved away from the

Bay Area, and he very much misses his rides on the ferry. Still, it is some satisfaction for him to know that there are others riding the ferry today with their binoculars in one hand and his Golden Gate Ferry checklist in the other.

It's doubtful that funds will soon come rolling in for this kind of project, and it likely will be even longer before we know the anwers to some of the intriguing questions about the seabirds' lives—obvious questions, like how they locate their food in the vastness of the sea. It's true that the seabird is on the top of the food chain, nobody eats a seabird, and there's no guano industry in California. But it's also true that a fisherman never beats the birds to the fish. In fact, even in this day of sonars and satellites, if it weren't for the seabird showing him the spot, the fisherman would lose a large percentage of his catch—that's talking millions of dollars of production in the state of California alone. And that's no guano!

Cormorant #45136

#45136 was banded as a chick on 9 August 1970. As is typical of Brandt's and other cormorants after fledging, #45136 wasn't seen again at the breeding colony on the Farallons until she was two years old. In 1972, she laid three eggs in her first nesting attempt, but it was in vain—all three of her eggs disappeared during their incubation period. For six of the next seven years, #45136 was one of two hundred birds watched by the Point Reyes group from the blinds in the rocks. By 1977, she had laid fourteen eggs and fledged five chicks. In 1978, the nutrient upwellings were late; only two Brandt's cormorants were able to feed well enough to produce an egg, and #45136 was one of them. By eight years of age she had produced twenty-six eggs and reared eight of them to independence. Actually, 31 percent breeding success is below average for a cormorant, but then #45136 had an outsized habit for switching mates and nesting sites.

Where she went during the winter when not nesting at the Farallons is difficult to say. However, from guesses based on 440 band recoveries from more than 7,000 banded cormorant chicks, she could have been traveling anywhere from central Baja to central British Columbia.

In November 1979, a San Francisco beach walker found a dead Brandt's cormorant with a band attached to its leg. The band was mailed to the U.S. Fish and Wildlife Service and then returned to the Observatory. At her death #45136 was the longest surviving banded bird in the study.

–paraphrased from Newsletter #54 Point Reyes Bird Observatory

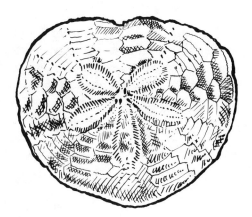

Chapter 21

All Things Small and Ugly

The closest I ever came to abandoning ship was off Moss Landing
while fishing halibut. This dark, indignant day began on the surface of a silky calm sea reflecting the pink of dawn, a cruel-fated
day that would so twist my perception of life on earth that I nearly
took the chance of leaving it. It was the second year that I had
fished and only the third or fourth time I had fished with a net.
The net was coming up as usual, with less fish than I had hoped
for, but not so bad as to warrant complaint: a handful of crabs, a
few rock cod, flounders, and not too far along the net, there was
the first halibut.

I flipped the halibut through one loop of the web and then back through the other, retrieving the fish from the net in the usual way. But already something was weird. This big, beautiful halibut was every bit a halibut except for the meat. There was skin, bones, head and tail, but not an ounce of flesh within. I knew it wasn't sand fleas or crabs that had made this work of art, because there wasn't the slightest violation of the fish's outer form. And I was certain it wasn't disease, because there's no way that this fish swam into the net in that condition. The puzzle was really stuck on my mind until I pulled a little more net and came up with a nasty roll of lead line and cork that required all my attention to unravel.

I took care of that mess, and up over the stern comes another halibut presenting the same enigma as the last. My hands were just about to grasp its tail when out of its orifice leapt a foot-and-a-half-long snake made out of snot, a god-awful serpent of slime. It dropped on the deck and writhed at my feet, crazed, like it was going to attack. I lurched backward, crashing against the gunwale, grabbed for my gaff, and began swinging maniacally at the beast. Over twenty times my gaff gouged deep puncture wounds into the wooden deck. But this terrifying creature was so fast and so maniacal and unpredictable that I missed the kill on every mind-jarring swing. The harrowing battle ended only when the serpent accidentally flipped itself down into the engine room through the door that, by the almighty grace of God, I had accidentally left open that morning.

I gasped and whimpered with relief, but slowly the terror resumed as I realized the Poe-like dimension and contour of my trap. I couldn't pull more net lest there be legions more snakes ready to seize the ship; I couldn't set the net back in the water because that meant standing by the engine room. I looked over my shoulder at the safety of the shore, only one little mile away — I would swim!

But inner bravery was crowned with outer will. From terror's paralysis, I moved one foot in front of the other until I got to the radio. "Mike!" I yelled, with a voice that rang with alarm.

"Look, take it easy," he began, in a very calming tone of voice; "you've got a slime eel on the boat. What you have to do is get two pieces of rope and tie them tight around your pants legs, because you can't have that thing crawling up you know where. You see what it did to the fish, don't you? HA, HA, HA, HA, HA, HA, HA, HA . . ."

My response came uncontrollably from a primitive heartless rage. "I hope the sharks tear you to shreds, you bastard, I hope . . ." I screamed at the top of my lungs.

But listen, now, to the story ten years later, for even as the lowly eel squirms mindlessly about on a slippery deck, so too the righteous postures of men take on the same sideways and slithering motion to proclaim beyond the necessity of words the oneness of all God's children. This by telephone.

"Hello, Mike? Do you still have your crab gear in the water?"

"Yeah, why? What's up?"

"I'm working on a book about the ocean, and I need to take a picture of a slime eel and—"

"A what? What are you, nuts?"

"Really, Mike, I want to show that there's more than dolphins in the ocean."

"So why don't you just take a picture of me? For Christ's sake, Marie, you've been on the beach too long."

"Look, Mike, why don't you just take a jar with a lid, keep it on the boat, and the next time you get a slime eel, just put it in the jar?"

"Oh, yuck, I don't want to be touching them things. And then what am I supposed to do? Bring it to my house?"

"Why not?"

"Well, you better be there to pick it up when I call you."

Even scientific discussions of the hagfish are replete with unscientific language—"repulsive-looking hags," "loathsome scavengers," "extremely ugly." But even the strictest language of science does little to enhance the acceptability of the lowly hagfish:

> a fish that has four hearts, only one nostril and no jaws or stomach; that can live for months without feeding; that performs feats of dexterity by literally tying itself in knots.

> the hagfishes are undoubtedly a very archaic form of life.

the hags burrow into their prey, usually dead or dying fish, leaving only a bag of skin and bones.

In its cocoon of slime the hagfish is almost impossible to grasp. Afterward [after the threat has passed], however, the animal must free itself of the slimy coat lest it suffocate because of blockage of its gills and nostril. The subtle hagfish accordingly loops its body into a half hitch, pulls itself through the loop and thus wipes off the slime.

These loathsome passages are taken from an article on slime eels in *Scientific American*. The author of this article is David Jensen, a heart specialist. The hagfish has four hearts and the beating of those hearts holds the secrets of the most primitive mechanisms of our own hearts, the wellspring of our very pulse, the deepest rhythm of our life. And if you're beginning to feel the first thin thread of attachment to this lowly eel, your long-lost blood relative, wait'll you hear this.

I was given the article from *Scientific American* by John McCosker at Steinhart Aquarium. I had gone there to use the library and ran into John in the hall. "What are you doing here?" he asked. And I told him I needed to look up slime eels.

"Slime eels?" He walked into the library. "There's this book here, and this one here, and let me get the article I have in my desk. Eels are my specialty."

And I thought to myself, Why *eels*, John? You're head of this whole aquarium, with a million different beautifully colored exotic fish. You could have your pick of specialization.

"While you're looking at this," said John, opening a book right to the page on slime eels, "I'll go get something that will blow your mind." And back he came with a deep brown leather billfold and a piece of soft blue leather. "This is the leather they use in making high-fashion dresses," he said. "It's expensive. You see these rows that look like stitches through the leather? That's the pattern from the back and sides of the slime eel," and John maneuvered the leather over the picture of the slime eel like a lifted fingerprint being held up to its master in the file. I was more dumbfounded than I've been in a long time. Can you believe it?

Slime eels are high fashion! "Right," said John. "They harvest them in Korea and import them into the U.S."

My God, I thought, wait till the fleet hears about this. A new fishery to save them from depletion. And when the time comes, Greenpeace can make a poster with a portrait of the slime eel where the harp seal used to be. How much support will Greenpeace get?

Chapter 22

A Question of Kindness

Congenital cataracts are one of those things nobody thinks is fair. And when the deep blue eyes of a fourteen-month-old become cloudier with each passing day, you can't just sit and do nothing. That's what this team of doctors and assistants felt, and that's why everyone in the operating room had volunteered his or her time. The drugs and instruments, too, were donated or paid for by people who felt the same way. The patient was already floating lightly on a mixture of halothane and oxygen, but still, it took seven people, heaving with all their might, to lift him onto the table. Behemoth was his name.

There are presently seventy pinnipeds being treated at the

California Marine Mammal Center in Sausalito on a budget of $159,000 a year that comes mostly from membership dues. California sea lions, harbor seals, stellar sea lions, and elephant seals are brought here from as far north as the Oregon border and as far south as San Luis Obispo. Below this point animals found ailing or stranded are generally taken to the Union Oil Animal Care Center at Marineland in Palos Verdes, a smaller center in the south that shares similar goals.

The California Marine Mammal Center was established in 1975 as a nonprofit organization. The first year they took in seven animals. In 1983, according to administrator Peigin Barrett, the center treated over four hundred animals for everything from abandonment, malnutrition, lungworm, and skin disease, to more exotic ailments like subcutaneous emphysema, a condition in which air leaks out of the lungs into tissues below the skin. One sea lion was blown up to such outsized proportions by this disease that during his stay the crew dubbed him "Michelin man."

In 1977, Peigin, who was then a writer and free-lance editor, started out as one of the dedicated volunteers who are the backbone of the organization. "The center is a rare opportunity," she says, "for people who want to work with wild animals. This is a hospital, but we maintain the animals wild so they can be returned to functioning in the wild. The center gives us the opportunity to study the animals' systems; it gives the seals a second chance; and it's a healing place for the people who work here as well."

Just through the daily treatment of the animals on a case by case basis, the staff is rapidly expanding our knowledge of pinniped biology and disease. Before these centers opened, nothing was known of the normal level of blood factors in sea lions; now they've been fully recorded. Diseases, like the elephant seal skin disease that starts in the flippers and eventually kills the animal, have been documented and treatments established. In the process of recording everything that comes through their doors, they're also beginning to spot trends, like the large number of tumors and parasites being found in the northern California sea lion, and then to look for causes.

There remains much to be learned about these animals. It's still not known exactly when they took their U-turn back to the sea;

fossil links are incomplete. But quite clearly, it was such a drastic change for mammals that had become entrenched on the land that every organ had to be reworked. They had to fatten up and streamline at the same time. Marine mammal mothers had to thicken up their milk so their babies could grow rapidly in the hostile ocean environment. Whereas land mammals rarely have a milk fat content higher than 12 percent, the milk of the Atlantic grey seal has a fat content of 53 percent. Because of these unheard-of nutritional requirements, young orphan seals brought to rehabilitation centers could not be sustained until someone came up with a brew of blenderized whipping cream and clams, guaranteed to tip the scales.

It is especially interesting that when these animals returned to the sea, they didn't retrace the evolutionary path on which they came out of the sea. The respiratory system had to readapt as much as any part of their bodies; yet there is no indication in any marine mammal of a trend toward gills or other mechanisms for pulling oxygen from water, despite the fact that some of them haven't touched land for sixty million years. Instead, they have developed completely new systems for allowing them to be underwater for long periods of time. The diving reflex is most notable, and it is based entirely on modifications of the land system. It involves the ability to shut down circulation to all but the most vital organs of the body, to drop the heart rate way below resting level, and to ignore the buildup of carbon dioxide as a stimulus to breathe. This diving reflex, combined with high levels of oxygen-carrying myoglobin in the muscles, allows some of these mammals to stay below for up to ninety minutes.

For all we have learned about our watery cousins, there are some rather obvious questions that continue to stump the boldest of speculators. For example: Where do marine mammals get their fresh water? From the fish they eat? True. Their kidneys excrete a lot of salt? True. But it still doesn't balance against their needs. The answers, of course, are swimming out there in the deep, far from human vantage.

Another segment of the ocean community, the commercial fisherman, would tell you, however, that some of these mammals are a little too close at hand. The sea lion, for one, hangs behind the fishing boat, waits till a salmon is hooked, eats the belly, tosses the rest of the fish in the air, and then goes down for the next one. "It's nothing for one sea lion to cost you up to a thousand dollars a day when the fishing's good, and that good fishing was supposed to cover all the bad days. There's only one way to get rid of them legally, and that's pass in front of another boat, and then you lose a friend along with the sea lion. It just doesn't make sense to spend hundreds of thousands of dollars treating animals that are over-populated, and the reason they're overpopulated is because people think they're cute and treat them like pets instead of wild ani-mals." This argument has never been one for quiet discussion, but since the passage of the 1972 Marine Mammal Protection Act it has been one of the most intractable and heated conflicts on the sea.

"The question somebody's got to answer," says Zeke Grader of the Pacific Coast Federation of Fishermen, "is how we are going to manage these animals. There's been a population explosion since the MMPA. The officials who enforce this thing know it, and they're telling us behind closed doors that we know how to take care of it. They're not the slightest bit worried about the size of the herds; they're worried about the environmentalists. So they're using the fishermen to be the gamekeepers out there. But it's not our duty to maintain the right population. It shouldn't be 'Well, we're going to look the other way, guys.' Sooner or later some group like Greenpeace is going to point the finger at us, and we're going to be made the bad guys and the management guys are going to get on the TV and say 'Oh, we think this is terrible.' Bullshit! They should explain to Greenpeace and the friends of the animals and all the other groups that they want to figure out a way to control the herds. Why shouldn't it be the Fish and Game out there doing the shooting, or giving them birth control pills, or putting them in jockey shorts, or whatever's got to be done? Sure, it's part of our culture to love the smart and the cute—but such an indulgence requires a responsibility. Besides, overpopulation leads to disease; it's nature's way of thinning the herd, of keeping the species strong. And now they want to cure that too."

It's been observed since 1971 that the California sea lions on their rookery at San Miguel Island and the Stellar sea lions at their rookery at the Farallons and the northern fur seals that breed at the Pribilofs are aborting a high percentage of their fetuses. Dr. Al Smith is a veterinarian currently at Oregon State University who has been looking at this problem from the start. One of the first clues to be pursued was the high levels of pesticides being found in the fatty tissues of the animals. Another possibility was a virus found in many pinnipeds that seemed more prevalent in the females that were aborting. As the years of study went on, it also became apparent that the rate of abortion among the seals was cyclical in nature; some years the rates would be very high, then they would drop back down for a while and then shoot back up again. "Disease is a very important and potent regulator of populations in the wild," says Dr. Smith, "and it's very hard to say whether something like this is a natural phenomenon or not, particularly with marine mammals of whom prior to the 1970s very few observations had been made. Disease profiles of marine mammals are poorly understood; in fact, there are only two types of viruses ever isolated from pinnipeds, and that's just ridiculous. It could very well be that these high abortion rates fluctuate with the food supply or with the density of the herd as a completely natural mechanism. It could also be that they are precipitated or exaggerated by the pesticides. There's no way we can say for certain without a whole lot more information."

As to whether these animals should be managed or left to the next hand of fate, Dr. Smith offered this perspective: "We're already managing them, just as nearly every other animal on earth is under some form of management. It comes down to whether you want animals or you don't want animals."

Behemoth was released at the Farallon Islands after he had been nursed back to a healthy weight. The animals are all tagged upon release for future reference, but so far Behemoth has not been spotted. Perhaps he fell victim to the social ostracism that greets relocated animals of so many species, or to the buckshot that came after an uncautious attempt to snag an easy fish from a fisherman's line. But given the dearth of observers over the great plains of the sea, it's just as likely that Behemoth is out there cavorting, hunting, and barking at the setting sun, and perhaps he has even courted himself a harem and squired a pod of lively pups, who are right now trying desperately to hunt for food through the growing cloudiness in their eyes.

Chapter 23

The Forest in the Sea

If in any country, a forest was destroyed, I do not believe nearly so many species of animals would perish as would here—from the destruction of the kelp.

Charles Darwin, 1834

Even from the window of your car, you can see the lush canopy of the most beautiful forest in the world—sensuous golden brown ribbons of kelp surging in the rocky shallows of the shore. Still, this surface beauty reveals little of the enchantment that lies below: life in all forms from top to bottom, dozens of species of colorful fish gliding in and out of the kelp that is anchored thirty to sixty feet down. And on the forest floor where the tendrils of kelp hold fast on the rocks, there live hundreds of different invertebrates spending their lives in the dense vegetation—kelp grazers like the urchin and abalone; critters of exquisite shape, like the sea stars and shrimps, their designs unencumbered by the rigid demands of gravity; lowliness crowned by stunning beauty, like the nudibranches, five centimeters of slug crawling on the blades of kelp, vested in fifty-kilowatt colors, reds, yellows, purples, polka dots, and stripes; and don't forget the lobsters, morays, and crabs living under the rocks. The towering forest undulates and bends in the surge, breaking the light that is already dancing from its passage through the prisms of surface waves. The fish come here to hide in the fronds and feed on the invertebrates and the detritus of decaying plants; the sea lions, sea otters, and other marine mammals come for the fish. One marine mammal comes here for every bit of it—the nudibranches, the fish, the forest, the light dancing through the kelp.

Every weekend you can see their cars parked along the highway by the sea, and you can see them on the beach, walking backward into the surf, tripping over their flippers, backward through thousands of years of evolution, trying to keep from getting spit back onto the beach by the breakers that reject and toss the human form as easily as an old piece of driftwood. Finally, there's a little lull in the surf, and a dozen black-suited sapiens return to the sea with only the red tips of their snorkels linking them to the air. Free as a bird in the sky and with a view that's just as good, they make their way to the forest, where they tuck their bellies, give one last splash of their fins, and disappear, not to be seen again for an hour. Every weekend, despite the bone-chilling cold of the Pacific waters, thousands of people don wet suits and return to the sea. California has the best diving in the world, and the kelp forests are the reason why.

Macrocystis is the scientific name for this plant that grows faster than any plant in the world (including bamboo). When conditions are right, the kelp can shoot up at the rate of two feet a day, photosynthesizing from the light of the sun on the canopy and absorbing nitrates and nutrients through their leaves in the water. Unlike land plants that have to get their food from roots, some water plants just soak it from the sea.

Kelp can be found from Alaska to Baja California, a solid resident of the California Current, though it rarely forms forests above Point Conception. The kelp beds of northern California are a slightly different species called *Nereocystis*, or more commonly, bull kelp, which is distinguished by having only a single float. One of the factors limiting its growth is the severity of winter storms, which can uproot young organisms or so tangle the sinuous blades of the larger plants that they rip themselves to shreds.

It's in southern California with its mild winters that the great forests of *Macrocystis* are sustained—thirty square miles of forest right off the beaches of Point Loma, another just as large off Palos Verdes, and forests that wreath the entire islands of Catalina and San Clemente. The advantage of the coastal forests is that you can drive right up to them, but if you take a boat to the islands you're guaranteed a great dive. If the sea is coming from the west, you can dive on the east side; if it's coming from the north, you dive on the south side. You rarely have to put up with a surge, the water is clean and clear, the beds are relatively pristine, the sea is warm—the best diving in the world! That's why any day of the week you can have your choice of dive boats to take you to the islands.

The lower temperatures of the north, however, haven't succeeded in freezing the spirits of the black-suited divers of northern California; nor has the poorer visibility, frequently less than fifteen feet, or the rougher waves. They push backward into the breakers with a little extra umph and gasp when first hit by the fifty- to sixty-degree water. "It's the same wet suit," they say, and disappear into the sea.

Diving isn't really a sport, any more than going to the mountains is a sport or taking off to a distant and unknown part of the world. It's the absence of land, stepping out of gravity for a while, and rolling, twisting, gliding through a strange, fluid element that opens the door on a whole new spectrum of possibilities. Just about anything you like to do on land you can do under water. Photography, hunting, meditating, exploring, competing, or just hanging out, but it's like doing it all in a kaleidoscope that seems to be perpetually turning around you.

Sharks? Troublesome sharks like blues and whites rarely come into a kelp forest; in fact, in all of California a shark bite occurs only once every four or five years. Of course, there's still that nagging fear that "if somebody's going to get bit, it's probably going to be me." But that's irrational, perhaps.

Buy a wet suit for a hundred dollars, mask, snorkel, and fins for another fifty, and you're in. Some of the best diving is in depths of less than twenty feet. So you really don't need scuba. But if you want to go deeper, it's open to anyone from age six to ninety-six; you don't have to be a jock. You do, however, have to be certified as a diver. Look in your phone book under dive shops. They're the centers of information—tours, classes, and people hanging out talking about diving—as well as the sellers of goods. California also has four active diving councils—north, south, central, and valley—that are involved in everything from diving medicine to protecting water quality to organizing underwater competitions. Their numbers and addresses are listed in the Marine Directory at the end of the book.

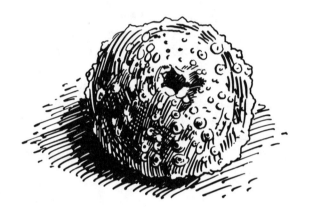

Chapter 24

The Mystery of the Disappearing Kelp

To the people of coastal Asia and the Pacific islands, sea plants are an important crop for food and medicines. They are harvested by the ton or, like a prize tomato, cultured in special ponds. In Japan over four hundred thousand people are supported by the industry. In Hawaii, over forty different kinds of "limu" are picked for a variety of uses and occasions. But on the mainland of the United States, sea plants are the slimy things you slip on at the tidepools. Except for one.

The canopies of kelp fronds are worth a million dollars per square mile, which alters the way we look at the kelp. There is algin in the cell walls of the kelp, a substance that allows the long leaf blades to stay resilient as they bend and twist in storms. Algin is also an emulsifier and is used in the stabilization of over seventy foods and medicines. A San Diego–based firm named Kelco is the largest harvester on the West Coast. They lease the major kelp beds of southern California from the Department of Fish and Game, an arrangement that may come as a surprise to those of you who think that only oil and gas interests take leases in the sea.

Kelco started back in 1929 with men hanging over the sides of the boats, pulling the heavy plants onto the boat with a long gaff, arm over aching arm, from morning till night. But business was good, and Kelco was inspired to build a better lawn mower with power-driven blades under the stern that cut a swath thirty feet wide three feet down and load it onto the boat with not much more effort than driving a golf cart over the greens. In the early 1960s Kelco harvested 155,000 tons a year. Now most of the crews are working shoreside, looking for new products to add to the sum; Kelco has over 140 people in the research department alone.

The sea urchin is a brainless echinoderm, a lowly little shell ball covered with hundreds of nasty spines to compensate for its inadequacies. It has lived on the floor of the kelp forest for a very long time, so long, in fact, that it has altered the design of other inhabitants of the forest. The red, white, and black sheepshead, the largest fish in the southern kelp, has two long, protruding buckteeth specifically designed for breaking into the urchin's shell; the lobster has its claws for the same purpose; and the sea otter was prompted for the same purpose to turn seabed rocks into tools. But the humans are only wracking their brains.

In the late 1940s, one of Kelco's divers noticed something interesting. He told the people at Scripps Institute that the urchins were grazing on the kelp. The people at Scripps said, "Can't be, they can't digest it." Kelco's diver insisted, "Maybe they can't, but they are." Scripps checked it out and, sure enough, found that the urchins did indeed have the enzymes to break through the cell walls of the kelp.

In the early 1950s, the kelp forests began dwindling, and this time Kelco called the scientists at Scripps for help. Right away they made a little bit of history; it was the first time that scientists worked with scuba on their backs. They placed transect lines on the forest floor and watched the movement of the urchins. (Transect lines are two ropes laid on the bottom in a cross configuration; they are the standard method for maintaining your point of reference while studying an underwater area.) Everyone was astonished at the findings: the sea urchins were advancing at the rate of thirty-three feet per month. Granted, it's not the Indy 500 down there, but to everyone involved these speeds were a dizzying indictment of the sea urchin's role in the disappearance of the kelp. Others weren't convinced because, at the same time, the City of San Diego sewer outfall was being discharged at a depth of thirty-five feet in San Diego Bay. The prevailing currents carried the sludge and muck north to the kelp beds. At the same time, there was a warming trend in the average ocean temperature, a phenomenon that drastically lowers the nutrient levels in the water. At the same time, people became aware that the sea otter that eats the urchins hadn't been around for half a century, and they also observed that the sea bass had been fished out and now the spearfishermen were going for sheepshead, the next largest fish in the beds. At the same time, pressure on the lobster fishery was more intense than ever before. Kelco had more answers than they knew what to do with. But by 1958, the harvest of kelp dwindled right down to nothing.

The study in the kelp bed had the same problem as most other studies in the ocean—the scientists were trying to explain the unusual without having any understanding of the usual. And the usual situation can never be understood, because it hasn't existed for decades and will probably never exist again. This kind of thinking, however, is a precious waste of time when you have a multimillion-dollar business going down the tubes. All brainpower had to be focused on a plan of action. Teams of divers were sent down into the kelp beds, armed with hammers. Day after day they smashed thousands of urchins to death. It worked about as well as the dustbowl farmers' attempts to combat the locust with the kitchen broom.

Research on the urchin continued in the laboratory. They found that the whole urchin is a bag of membranous spines capable of absorbing amino acids from sewage. Kelp, on the other hand, doesn't do well in sewage. Those pointing their fingers at the sewage pointed to places where sewage had been removed and the kelp had come back. Friends of the sewage pointed to places where there was no sewage and the kelp had disappeared anyway. Friends of the Sea Otter said, You see what happens when you take an animal out of the top of the food chain? They wanted to bring the furry urchin eater back to the southern kelp beds, but that went over with the abalone fishermen about as well as a campaign in Petaluma to bring back the wolf. Only the quicklime was irrefutable.

In 1962, a scientist put eight hundred pounds of quicklime in Abalone Cove at Palos Verdes. The urchins were eliminated, and the kelp grew back. A solution, at last! The scientists and Kelco began spreading tons of quicklime in the kelp beds to destroy the urchin. But then the Department of Fish and Game came along and said, Hey, we have to relegate the use of chemicals in the ocean. So the scientists and Kelco and Fish and Game spread tons of regulated quicklime on the kelp forest for years and years. Quicklime only kills echinoderms and a few mollusks, animals like urchins, sea cucumbers, starfish, abalones, and so on.

Kelco also put a lot of energy into developing a market for the urchin. Commercial harvesters are now taking the large red urchin, which is a delicacy to the Japanese. Production has been so good, in fact, that the growing numbers of urchin fishermen demanded a stop to the quicklime. The last year the kelp beds were sprayed was 1980. Finally, the urchins had found a friend, but the story didn't end there.

In 1983, there wasn't a harvestable frond of kelp in all of southern California. Some say the warm waters of the aberrant El Niño current completely demolished the crop. Others say the catastrophe wouldn't have been so bad if the kelp beds had been in a healthier state. But "Friends of the Journalists" say, Please give us a break.

Chapter 25

El Niño

I could tell you about the tropical barracudas gliding around the Farallon Islands; or I could tell you about the islands themselves —cold, jagged rocks that for centuries have gritted against the lashings of a murky green sea, condemned to ghosthood in the gray fog, a lonely chain of rocks that everyone agrees were put there by God for the misery of fishermen. And now, suddenly, as if in reward for a job well done, He is blessing them in a bath of warm, clear southern water and a halo of unseasonal sun. But this warm current called El Niño has spawned far stranger tales than these, stories that reach beyond the depths of the seas into the cavernous hearts of men.

This one starts three thousand miles to the east in Washington, D.C., in 1976. The Two-Hundred-Mile-Limit Bill was passed by Congress, and the territory of the American dream was extended by as many horizons of sea. "Westward ho," said the men from the East, and the fishermen rejoiced in the promise of the day.

They had had it with the huge fleets of foreign ships—from Russia, from Japan, from Poland, from Korea—300-foot ships that in one tow of their gigantic nets could take more fish than any of our small vessels could catch in a year. And if our fishermen were foaming about that situation, they were whipped into a full raging gale by our government's insistence that these foreign ships were only taking the hake. "Who are they trying to kid?" said the fishermen. "Even our own drag boats get salmon in their nets, and the speed of our drag boats is nothing compared to those ships. And they're going to make us believe they don't catch salmon and rock cod and everything else that swims in the water? Sometime taste the water after one of those ships has passed, and you'll see that even the salt is gone."

Could it be that after a century of neglect the government was actually responding to the fishermen's plea? Two hundred miles of protection was an omen to behold!

Nineteen seventy-six, and it finally began to dawn on the rugged, centuries-old multimillion-dollar fishing industry that "this politics, this lobbying, whatever you call it" might very well prove to be a useful part of the business. The Pacific Coast Federation of Fishermen was formed, and Zeke would be at the helm.

For a number of years now, Zeke had successfully managed his dad's fish dock—unloading boats, filleting fish, wholesaling, hosing down the slime, and maintaining equanimity among the oceanic moods of the fishermen. "Zeke's not afraid to get his hands in a little slime," they joked. "He ought to do real well up there in Sacramento."

He was smart, too, and had just graduated from law school he had been attending at night. Sure, he was a little young, "but don't think for a minute that old Dad won't be working right by his side." "Dollar Bill," as they called his dad around the docks, had the aura of a whale. He was the first person to break into the California fish buying business whose last name didn't roll off the tongue like a Verdi opera. The Tarantinos, Puccinis, Aliotis, Lazios, and Palladinis had held the California coast for themselves until Bill came along. Anyone who could get along with the *famigli* for thirty years must know a lot of moves. Nobody doubted Bill's ability to handle whatever problem might come up.

At the same time, PCA moved into full swing—Production Credit Association, the government agricultural loan agency, decided the time was ripe to enter the fish business. They began sending guys in shiny shoes down to the docks, soliciting. "How do you do, Mr. Fisherman, how would you like a new boat? A faster boat, a deeper, sturdier, handle-better-weather, catch-more boat?"

"By golly," said the fishermen, "the government is even putting its money where its mouth is!"

And then came the PFMC, Pacific Fisheries Management Council, some kind of federal committee that met somewhere on the beach to oversee the fisheries; nobody really had too much idea what they were up to, and not too many cared. After all, in all the years Fish and Game had supervised this thing, they never did much more than check for undersized crabs in the crates.

And in what seemed like no time at all, Jack the accountant arrived on the scene. Debbie, the assistant in Zeke's new office, was married to Jack. She decided to help her husband start up his accounting business by handing out his card to whichever fisherman passed her desk.

The timing was perfect. The fishermen fluffed out their wings and hailed him aboard for the ride, just like the hunter pelican with the seagull following on every beat of his wings. You could hear the pride on the radio in the fishermen's daily chatter. Amid discussions of water color, upwellings, wave heights, yesterday's catch, Joe's bum move, the price at the dock, recipes, and the stories of days gone by, every once in a while now, you'd hear a golden-ringed reference to "my accountant." My accountant says this and my accountant says that. "He takes care of all my headaches. After all these years, he even got the tax board off my back." "You mean Jack? Hey, I got him too. A lot of these guys are out here breaking their balls, not realizing what Jack can do with a little paperwork." In the beckoning radiance of civilization, the fishermen weren't thinking about the things they already knew, like how poorly their vision was adapted to land, that once removed from the lucidity of infinite blue, they couldn't tell the pelicans from the sea gulls from the sharks. Besides, on a heyday like this was turning out to be, you just harvest for all you got.

It got so they even consulted Jack like an oracle—about a depreciation schedule before selling a net, about their tax bracket before making the next trip. And if you wanted a law changed, you went up to Zeke's office and helped him put a meeting together with a real senator; if you wanted a radar, you just rang up PCA.

To top everything off, the glow of the times was being matched by the bounty of the sea. The oceanic upwellings make northern California waters one of the richest fisheries on earth. The severe northwest winds churn the cold, nutrient laden waters from the deep up to the surface where the light of day is like the touch of a wand, creating vast areas of plankton bloom from Point Conception all the way up the California coast. The fields of plankton bring the herring and anchovies and they in turn bring massive schools of rock cod, salmon, mackerel, halibut, tuna—as great a diversity of fish as can be found anywhere in the world. And these years the upwellings were producing at their healthiest.

As in all years past, the fishermen roamed the ocean for days at a time, nomads in search of these spots of upwelling that change as abruptly as the winds—only now they loaded their boats! Trip after trip after glorious trip, showered in the fountains of life! *Madre di Dio!* It was quite a couple of years!

And when the winds got so bad that even the rugged cedar- and oak-framed boats couldn't take the punishment, the fishermen tied them to the docks, hauled out the barbecues and fish, watermelons, wine, friends, and "let 'er blow!" The sheer volume of the catch that can be produced by the sea fires the delirium of hitting the main vein, and the sea stories wind into the reckless hours of the night.

Still, even in these days, there was a back eddy to the flow, a deep persistent countercurrent pumping beneath the depths. Pretty much all the guys had long since been to their last meeting, flabbergasted even by the process itself. "How many years have I been reaching into that water, and they think because I didn't go to biology school, I don't know the ocean. I don't need to waste my time and get insulted too. And the politicians? Hell, they made their hand clear way back in 1976 when the first thing they did with that bill was hand out complimentary tickets to the foreign ships. And everything they done since says the name of the game is minerals and oil. If we gotta dance to that kind of music," said the fishermen, "then may nature take her course."

But even before 1976, there were signs that the fishermen sensed their way of life would be sacrificed to the ways of the land. Even two decades ago, fathers no longer brought the young boys of the family onto the boats, no matter how much the child pleaded and begged. The fishermen wouldn't even allow the kids to mend the nets for fear that the rhythm alone would hook the kids to the sea. It was always with the most unbearable ache of sadness that the fathers broke the chain of generations and abandoned the child to the land. But they knew the days of the sea were numbered.

Still, none of this was reason enough to stop a party. When your number's up, it's up, and when it's time to eat, drink, and be merry, you shouldn't be worrying about the little things. A big catch, a bad wind, and another barbecue was open to all. So, "Come on, Zeke, put another steak on Ginger's plate; don't you know a little dog like that could starve just from the lack of one meal?" "Hey, now listen, Jack, old buddy, if I could find fish the way you inclinate to a party, your bill would have been paid long ago."

April 1983, the fifty-fourth annual opening of the commercial salmon season. The boats were readied and the fishermen set off for another year of work that is grueling, rugged, and treacherous no matter what the take of fish. Scout the massive rolling seas west of the point, buck out to the Bodega Canyon, radio the guys off Eureka, spend a couple of days taking a beating at the Farallons where there's always a couple of kings haunting the rocks and stalking the bait. And everywhere the reports were unbelievable! The fertile expanse of murky green waters was displaced from horizon to horizon by crystal blue water, beautiful in its clarity and warmth, repellent in its absence of life. No plankton, no feed, no fish! And the Farallons? Haven of hundreds of thousands of seabirds squawking in frenzy over the swarms of bait, an incessant screeching choir, so loud and piercing through the dark, gray mists that the crews of the boats that work there know more of underworlds and demons than they do of the California sun? This great rock sat immersed in a sparkling blue bath looking like it should be a retreat for the gods and issued naught but the quiet of a tomb.

Only the fishermen called out their distress, looking for a good word on the fish. And over the full length of the coast only "El Niño" was uttered, like a curse.

The name was no stranger to the fishermen. It had long ago lost its innocence in the waters of Peru—a name passed halfway across the globe and up through generations in the fishermen's tales of misery past, a deadly rogue current from the equator that destroyed the anchoveta and the whole Peruvian economy in one scalding lap of its tongue. A failure of the trades, a shift of the Pacific high, an atmospheric perturbation, whatever—the upwellings of life were snuffed and stagnant. The stories of El Niño were humbling enough, but to actually have that water wrapped around your keel for mile after smothering mile, to run for days to any point on the compass, then look over the side and see the same rays of sun flashing like swords in the crystalline blue, as if the whole ocean were a liquid star sapphire and you could never escape its lifeless eye. Even the most jaded old-timers were stunned.

In a matter of weeks the entire fleet was tied to the dock, save for the handful of boats sent to scout. The weeks turned eerily to months. There was a flurry of boat sales, but pretty soon even the doctors and lawyers looking for tax write-offs went searching for better grounds. The number was up. The fish, the fishermen, the industry—"That's it, boys, the era is done." There was no rush to Zeke's office to file for government relief, and not much cause to see Jack at all. At the very least, it was an era that died with its boots on. No bypass operations, no artificial heart.

Of the guys who are left, the ones whose boats were paid for, they're keeping a low profile or eking out a meal on the halibut. Then there are those who just really believe that as long as the ocean is deep, it will continue to astonish. And one day, there it is, a whole netful of something you never saw before. "You wouldn't believe what I got here," he calls to his buddy. "I got a netful of skinny sharks. Ain't that something, even the sharks get skinny." And he laughs that irrepressible laugh of a man who knows he can reach in the water with his bare hands and touch on the most amazingly simple truths.

And Jack says, "I told Zeke to get a grant, it's so damn easy. I told him two years ago, this business of trying to support the organization off assessments on the fish was ludicrous. It's their own fault; you gotta run this thing like a business of the century you're in. And when Debbie did all that work on that exhibit up there at the Sacramento fair and Charlie Fullerton came over with the TV cameras following right on his heels, what did they say over at the office? They said, why is she up there wasting our time? All they want to do is lobby like the old days. There's a big gap to reality there. Don't they see what the milk people did?"

Down at Zeke's office the long table in the conference room is stacked with reports, letters in progress, memos, briefs, an incredible network of communication with every part of the world that touches on fisheries, with people diving in and out of it like birds on a school of bait. The chairs are covered in the same way, and so are the floors and coffee table. The surface of Zeke's desk hasn't been seen since the day the office opened. The phone's ringing off the hook, and it's probably the building manager, because next month's rent is still waiting for fish to cross the dock. Zeke did go looking for grants, and in the final blow to his efforts, Small Business Administration Chief James Sanders said that El Niño did not meet the agency's definition of a natural disaster. The Reagan administration did, however, come up with $100 million in El Niño aid to Bolivia, Peru, and Ecuador.

Only the Pacific Fisheries Management Council is unparched in the midst of this scorching drought of droughts. Fed by the wellsprings of Washington three thousand miles to the east, they continue flying their scientists up and down the coast, setting up new committees, buying more computer time, consulting more statisticians, and writing increasingly complicated fisheries management plans on the majestic king salmon, which over the full length of the Pacific coast is nowhere to be found.

Jack is standing arms folded in his new office, which has been diversified for corporate accounts. "It's sad," he says, in a rare somber mood, and he shakes his head, staring deep into the lush new carpet. "It's really, really sad." Because Jack was in it for the same reasons as everyone else: to tap the nectar of the fertile up-wellings of our own backyard, to feel the rise of the swell, to ride in the sparkling foam of the crests—for the sheer roll of it. Man's ancient desire to play his hand on the helm of fate, with the careless whims of the child.

Chapter 26

Portrait of a Fisherman

Freckles is a California fisherman who has worked the ocean for sixty-one of his sixty-eight years. He has fished for anchoveta off Peru, for sardines off Mexico, for tuna out of San Pedro, for mackerel, crab, shark, herring, salmon, sea bass, albacore, rock cod, pompano, flounder, halibut—all along the coast all the way up to Alaska. As he says, he's worn out more pairs of boots than shoes.

In addition to mending nets, navigating the boat, repairing rigging, and working the gear from dawn to dusk, Freckles, like all other successful fishermen, is a keen naturalist. Fishermen are the only people who spend their lifetimes daily reaching into the ocean's depths, the accuracy of their observations and intuitions being continually tested against the severest measure of all—how much food they can bring to the family table. Fishermen don't get paid for putting in time. It is the single greatest loss to our understanding of the ocean that the great majority of scientists and ocean officials consider fishermen to be ignorant because they never went to school. This attitude has been frustrating and maddening to the men of the sea, but it has never diminished their view of themselves. "They think I'm stupid," says Freckles, "but they'll never convince me I'm stupid. I forgot more about the ocean than all their biologists put together ever knew."

The lives of the fishermen have been far too rich to harbor bitterness for very long—rich in experience, in extremes, in freedoms, in beauty, and in community—a community of people more strongly bonded than any that have formed on land, welded on a single keel of dedication to keeping each other alive and consecrated around a galley table of feasts and sharing of tales. The sea story, as every fisherman knows, is his richest harvest of all.

The incident Freckles tells about here took place in the 1950s while he and his cousin Dominic were fishing for sea bass in the waters off Stinson Beach. For the first time anywhere, it links a homegrown, down-on-its-luck white shark to Jaws, the most infamous monster of them all.

"We lay the nets off Stinson Beach on a Friday afternoon, and Saturday morning we picked them up. The sea bass were thick. We loaded up with sea bass, leopard sharks, soup fin sharks, and three big white sharks. Naturally, we threw the white sharks back in the water; then we cleaned the fish, laid the nets back out, and here comes the Fish and Game. But what we were doing was legal.

"Fish and Game boarded us and started measuring the nets that had damage and looking around, and they asked us if we had any salmon.

" 'What salmon?' I said. 'You see any salmon? If you want to check the boat, go ahead and check the boat.' When he was finished, I said, 'Look, pal, you'd better put an alert on that there's a lot of man-eaters here, the ones that have four, five rows of teeth.' The warden looked at me like I was a salami. I said, 'They're all over the place near the swimmers. The only reason you don't see them is because they don't very often fin on top of the water like other sharks.'

"He asks, 'How big?'

"I said, 'Maybe twelve to fourteen feet. We had one so big we had to chop him with a machete, to say nothing of the net he took with him.'

"Fish and Game says, 'Aren't you exaggerating about these man-eaters?'

"I said, 'How am I going to prove it? If you don't believe me, go to hell.'

"So we did our chores; we ate, mended the damage, and anchored for the night. Sunday morning, as we pulled the nets, I see helicopters, boats, and cruisers all over the area. What's all this commotion? Maybe some boat is missing. We didn't know what was going on.

"We kept working and had another big heavy day. We had one small white shark about eight feet long come up in the net. I told my cousin, 'Put the sling on the son of a bitch.'

"Dom says, 'What the hell are we going to do with it? We're not going to get any money for him. What are you doing?'

"So I told him, 'I'm going to bring it into the city and stick it down the Fish and Game's throat.' Because, see, it was bugging me that Fish and Game said I was exaggerating.

"We left the few nets that weren't damaged in the water and headed back to the wharf to deliver. We went by the ferry slip. The whole gang was there and they were clapping. I thought it was because the boat had a big list and was down in the water from the weight of the fish. I thought they were glad because it looked like a new fishery. We had no way of knowing what had happened the day before. I pulled alongside Standard Fisheries, and Sam from the shellfish market was there. 'Ah,' he says, 'you got the shark! You got the one!'

" 'Yeah, I got one,' I said. 'Who knows how many we got. There's too many sharks, too much damage to the nets.'

"Sam says, 'They've been looking for that shark since Saturday.'

" 'This shark?' I says. 'Not *this* shark.'

" 'Yeah, the Coast Guard's looking for him. Everybody's looking for him. That shark ate the kid. The kid was swimming at

Baker's Beach, and a big white one got him and took half his shoulder.'

" 'But there's a million of these sharks,' I said. 'They're all over the place out there, you just don't see them. They're on the bottom.'

"Right away Fish and Game and everybody came down to the wharf. They wanted to see the shark. They actually thought this was the shark that ate the kid.

"Later that day while we were mending my gear, my friend Jiggs, another fisherman, comes up to me and says, 'Those scientists who took the shark want you to go down to the California Academy of Sciences.'

"I said, 'What for?'

" 'They want to ask you about the shark.'

"I said, 'Look, Jiggs, we got damage and we've still got gear laying in the water. I'm not going to be going monkeying around with those professors and doctors.'

" 'Freckles, you got to be there at two thirty, at the Academy of Sciences in Golden Gate Park.'

"So, the three of us, Jiggs, Dom, and I, were in Golden Gate Park going around and around and around. Lost! I don't know how many times we went around and every time we ended up at the Cliff House. I was so pissed. We lost a whole day with this shark. I was sure sorry I ever winched the thing aboard.

"We arrived late; they had already started and were looking at the blowups of the kid's picture and studying the teethmarks of the shark, which they had already cut up into a million pieces. In the stomach, they found beer cans, rocks, license plates, salmon, crabs, sea bass—eighty-eight pounds of undigested fish. One of the large salmon you could have put right in the market. There wasn't even a scratch. The shark must have swallowed him whole.

"This guy that was supposed to be a professor of fisheries was talking and he says, 'The coast is being invaded by these sharks from New Zealand.'

"I started laughing out loud. Dom starts poking me to quit laughing. I said, 'But, Dom, he's going to try to make me believe these sharks came from New Zealand? That we never had them here before?'

"So I stood up and I told the professor, 'No offense, but how do you know this shark comes from New Zealand? Has he got a dog tag like the soldiers? Ever since I've been a kid, we've had these sharks here. The only thing is we get them tangled in the nets, we kill them and we let them go.'

"I couldn't put it in this guy's head. He thinks I'm stupid because I'm a fisherman. He kept believing they came from New Zealand. So I told him again, 'Every year in the latter part of July, August, September, October, you get the man-eaters all the time, right up to the beach. They're nothing but a nuisance to us.' But this guy wouldn't listen.

"At least I learned something that day; about the teeth of the shark replacing themselves, that they urinate through their skins, and they carry rocks for ballast. These things I learned because I'm not a biologist, but he sure isn't going to tell me we're being invaded from New Zealand.

"Two years later I was helping my son-in-law cook crabs in his restaurant. This guy came over to me, a young fellow, and he says, 'Can I pick your brains a little on the shark?'

"'What shark?' I said. I didn't connect right away, because it was over two years and there'd been a lot more sharks in between. He asked me where I caught it, how I caught it, every last detail, the whole story.

"I said, 'What's this all for?' And he claimed he was going to write a book. I didn't think anything of it after that. After all, he didn't say, 'I'll give you some money when it comes out.'

"Three years later the book came out. Then comes the movie, and the movie was *Jaws*."

Chapter 27

Fishing for the Fun of It

Just because things aren't like they used to be is no excuse. If you can't hook a fish wherever you throw your line in California waters, it's because your attitude is wrong, or you're using the wrong bait, or the cows are on the wrong side of the pasture.

Lesson #1: The fish are down there — around the rocks, coves, piers, reefs, kelp beds, and in the mud. Along the full length of our beautiful, diverse coast, California is good fishing. And some of the best spots are perpetually unattended; just because there are no fishermen in an area doesn't mean there are no fish.

Lesson #2: Hang out with other fishermen. Find the local bait shop that has the big coffeepot, and beer in the fridge with the bait. This will be the same bait shop where the fishermen hang out and lie to each other. Listen intently to the local scoop—which fish is running, who caught what where, the latest theory on the effect of rainbows on the feeding habits of bass in the late afternoon lagoon. Put in your two cents, ignore all of it, and then go fishing.

Lesson #3: The key to finding a good spot is good faith, relentless observation, and one strict, unbreakable rule—don't ever allow a conclusion to become fully jelled in your mind. You've observed that the reef fish bite on the start of the incoming tide; it even makes sense, because on the outgoing tide, they're in a hurry to vacate the area so as not to get trapped in a waterless pond. Don't ever let something like that become a complete thought; don't ever put the period on the end of the sentence. Otherwise, the very next day you won't be able to buy a fish on the incoming because they already ate on the outgoing. Rock fish don't like the sand; sharks feed during slack water; perch love shrimp; salmon get aggressive in the fall; herring like little silver lures; tuna stay in the blue water; bass work the rips. You have to know every bit of it, and actively *not* know it, both at the same time, with a singular righteous passion laced with a devil-may-care approach. This is why so many people love fishing; it's a classic altered state of mind.

Me? I love *catching* fish. And I wasn't about to put up with all this ritual and voodoo, especially when I saw that this guy's voodoo was different from that guy's voodoo, and it didn't seem to make the tide turn one way or another. Then I began to notice that a very few guys always get 'em, no matter what. So I checked out their voodoo and was further disconcerted: one guy who gets 'em all the time has the opposite voodoo from the other guy who gets 'em all the time. "Silver lures when the sun is shining through a cloudless sky," said one. "Whatever you do, don't use silver when the sun is shining," said another. "You gotta think like a fish," said one. "All you gotta do is leave your line in the water," said the other. Self-canceling voodoo was all I could see—except for their buckets full of fish. So I continued to observe these people who always get 'em no matter what, and that's when I realized about the altered state of mind—the nature of reality in a fluid medium, fact as it's filed in the surge, serendipity as it's cast in the sea, truth as it turns in the tide, voodoo as the only rational hook. And then I noticed that the guys who always get 'em no matter what would sometimes have streaks of weeks or even months when they couldn't buy a fish if their lives depended on it. Which only convinced me more. There is no rhyme or reason; there is total rhyme and reason.

Lesson #4: Gear is your communication with the fish. It must always carry two messages—irresistible deliciousness and invariable lethalness. Neither of these is obtained by buying a lot of expensive, flashy silver, copper, luminescent chrome, particularly if it turns you on. It was designed to turn you on; it was not designed to turn on the fish. Everybody knows this stuff is for catching fishermen, not fish. But as soon as you walk in the gear store and the flash hits you between the eyes, it fires off a primitive ganglion in your nerves, and in the midst of the seizure, you observe your hand reaching out for the lure. It's most important as you walk through a gear store to repeat the following mantra: Any coastal fish in California can be caught with under ten dollars' worth of gear—a hook, a line, and a sinker.

The right hook, line, and sinker, to be sure, all tied together with the right knots. Any knot that slips or breaks is the wrong knot; any lead that doesn't put the bait right at the level of the fish's face is the wrong lead; any hook that goes into the fish's mouth and doesn't hook is the wrong hook. Which, though all this doesn't cost a lot, does require some thoughtful consideration of the extensive variables, from the size of the fish, to the surge and the currents and the local effect of the moon. The actual rigging of the line has to be done properly, too. You can slide the weights or you can attach them securely. You can go with the theory that light lines work best, or you can figure that heavy gear will never break. Or you can walk up to the counter and tell the man where you're planning to fish and what you want to catch. Tell him you want six of the right hooks, six of the right leaders, six of the right leads, and two hundred feet of the right line—and don't forget the swivels. Now it's just too embarrassing to stand there and ask him to tie it for you, too. So here are two examples of ways to tie your gear, just to get you started.

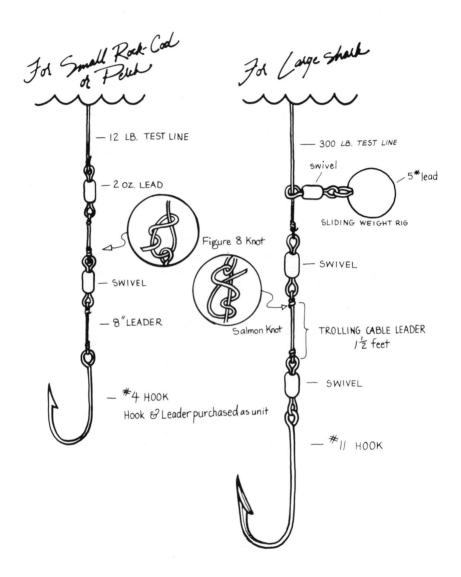

For Small Rock-Cod or Perch

— 12 LB. TEST LINE

— 2 OZ. LEAD

Figure 8 Knot

— SWIVEL

— 8" LEADER

— #4 HOOK
Hook & Leader purchased as unit

For Large Shark

— 300 *LB. TEST LINE*

swivel

— 5# lead

SLIDING WEIGHT RIG

— SWIVEL

Salmon Knot

TROLLING CABLE LEADER
1½ feet

— SWIVEL

— #11 HOOK

Lesson #5, catching the fish: You've arrived, sitting on the dock of the bay, stretched on a sea-splashed rock, or sunk up to your knees in the salt marsh, and they're not bitin'. Patience is exemplary, but it will never catch a fish where there are no fish. Move around a little and take a different approach. Consider the tides, underwater contour, what happened yesterday, the behavior of the fish, the natural feed in the area; then scan the territory and pick a better spot. As likely as not, this will stimulate some action for the fishermen who exercised their patience and stuck to your original spot. Don't be embarrassed about walking right back in their midst and dropping your line right beside them. It's the highest form of flattery.

The bait swings out over the water, drops below the surface, and bam, you got one. Don't let the fish get away! Kill it before you remove the hook so it won't jump back into the water; then rebait your hook and get it right back in the game. Now, look at your fish. You never saw one like this before? Keep it. Keep and eat everything you take from the sea, unless it's illegal or undersized. Eels, sharks, skates—they're all delicious. The only problem you may encounter is that a very few fish (like the golden croaker) have internal organs that, if broken, can put a bitter taste in the meat. So if you don't recognize your fish, just be careful as you fillet not to cut into belly organs. If you've never eaten fish that wasn't store-bought, you're in for a tasty surprise. The flavor of fish dissipates almost as rapidly as its color. There is nothing in the world like the wild, sweet taste of a fresh-caught fish. Once you've had a couple of your own meals, you'll be hooked.

Chapter 28

Recipes for Trash and Incidental Fish

Over 50 percent of the fish delivered to our docks are used as fertilizer or exported to other countries. What's even more astounding is that much of the fish caught by our fleet never even make it to the dock. They're thrown back into the water—dead! Aside from this fate, trash and incidental fish have one other thing in common—they're some of the best-tasting and most nutritious food in the world. This tragic waste of readily available seafood is proving very difficult to remedy. It's deeply rooted in the fishermen's economic situation, the buyer's outdated facilities, the American public's ignorance of seafood, and the anatomy and behavior of the fish itself.

In the past decade, various government agencies, including National Marine Fisheries Service, West Coast Fisheries Development Fund, and Sea Grant, have focused large amounts of money and effort on this problem with only minimal success. One of the first obstacles that became apparent is that each fish is its own unique case; you unravel the problem for one kind of fish and it doesn't help the other fish in the slightest. So what follows here are five different stories for five different fish, each with a recipe, all of them equally delicious.

Anchovy: I know; you've already tasted anchovies, on the top of your pizza, and they're too damn salty. What you probably don't realize is that the pizza anchovy is highly processed, and the taste bears no resemblance to that of an anchovy fresh from the sea. The taste of a fresh anchovy, in fact, is indistinguishable from a sardine. Both fish occupy the same plankton-grazing niche in the ocean food chain. In the late 1940s when the California sardine fishery collapsed, the anchovy moved in and took its place in the ocean—but not in the marketplace. People were too puckered up from the pizza anchovy to bite. But one old fish buyer had been in the business too long to be discouraged by a little problem like that. He simply canned the anchovies, attached the old sardine label, and tried his best to keep up with the demand. Till one day the FDA paid him a little visit.

The sardines you get at the grocery store today are imported from Spain, Portugal, or South America. And the eighty thousand tons of anchovies caught every year off the coast of California are ground into fish meal to feed the chickens. Chickens are so overbred they can taste manufactured, anchovies are as wild as they come; chickens are fed drugs and hormones, anchovies are so low on the food chain they take up even less pollutants than other ocean fish; chickens are over a dollar a pound, anchovies are twenty cents a pound. But the catch is that anchovies can rarely be found at your local fish market. Most likely you'll need to take a bucket to the dock, where a fisherman is likely to fill it for free.

Then take the anchovies home and do what the fishermen do. Break out the wine, invite your friends, and light up the barbecue. Cut the bellies of the fish and, in one sweep with spoon or fingers, remove the innards. Place the anchovy, head, fins and all, on the barbecue. In a matter of minutes the anchovy is cooked. Pick it up by the head and eat the rest of the fish like a crisp potato chip. Repeat the procedure until the fish or the wine is gone. And they're not salty!

Shark: Shark is eaten in nearly every country of the world that has a seacoast. So why not in America? It's an especially puzzling question because so many of our ancestors came from countries in which fish like shark, anchovies, herring, to name just a few, were considered staples, if not delicacies. Somewhere along the line we developed a "beef" mentality. Still, I'll bet you've not only eaten shark but paid dearly for it, too, and very possibly, you even sent compliments to the chef. Many of the best seafood restaurants are keenly aware of the quality of shark. They serve it as the white meat on the captain's plate, or put it in their cioppino and bouillabaisse; an especially profitable switch is the old shark to swordfish trick, which works out quite well because they are so alike in taste and texture. About the only place you won't see shark is on the menu. Skate, another member of the elasmobranch family, is used in the same way, except that skate tends a little more toward the flavor of crab, so sometimes it gets used at the crab canneries. There is also a cookie-cutter apparatus around for cutting skate wings and "making" scallops. It always amazes me when I see people fishing off the dock and throwing back freezer-size skates and shark after five-pound shark and then start jumping up and down yelling at their friends to come take a look when they hook into a little rock cod the size of a hot dog.

There are two very bad consequences of this nonsense. One, the fishermen get paid next to nothing when they deliver shark; and two, the public is deprived of low-cost, high-quality protein that, in addition, has another unique advantage: both shark and skate have no bones! As for taste, not much has to be said for an animal that can so routinely be substituted for swordfish. Prove it to yourself. Buy a few filets from one of the markets that are now beginning to handle shark, or catch one off the nearest pier. Throw it in the frying pan with nothing to molest it except perhaps a little lemon juice and butter.

One thing you should know if you catch your own: Shark has a high urea content in the skin, so clean it right away to keep the urea from seeping into the meat.

Hake: Of all the underutilized species, hake is the only one that has a severe character defect of its own contributing to its lack of use. Hake is plagued with not one, but numerous, forms of ugliness—ugly to look at, ugly to handle, and ugly to think about. They're a shit-brown, jaundiced-eyed school fish looking for their favorite blooms of plankton, also colored brown. They are caught in large numbers incidental to dragging, netting, or trolling (you're never lucky enough to catch just one hake, their schools are so thick), and you hear about it because the fisherman immediately gets on his radio to broadcast his disgust. Even among fishermen, who know that everything in the sea is fitting fare for the main course of a meal, hake is a four-letter word. So when the National Marine Fisheries Service estimated that the west coast of the United States would sustain an annual hake harvest of 175,000 metric tons, there was no rush on the gear stores. Fortunately, two white fillets of meat that run down either side of the fish kept the subject from being dropped. That, plus the potential volume, plus the fact that another species of hake was being eaten in Australia, encouraged the West Coast Fisheries Development Fund to put four hundred thousand dollars into solving the problem of taking the mush out of the hake. Nowhere is as far as they got.

Then Bruce Wyatt called up Jerry Barton. Bruce is the Marine Extension Agent for Sonoma County, and he knows that sometimes, even more than money, a problem needs just the right person. Jerry used to be a biologist, and her husband, Bob, used to be an engineer. Together, Bob and Jerry built the *Sea Trek*, a husky 42-foot troller, and have been fishing salmon, albacore, herring, crayfish, and shrimp for the last twenty years, all the time experimenting on their own with everything from the gear to the marketplace. Bruce scrounged up a meager thirty thousand dollars in grant money, enlisted the services of a properly equipped drag boat, and spent day after day at sea testing the best way to handle these fish on the boat to keep their texture firm. Jerry supplied her kitchen and her savvy as she experimented with hundreds of recipes, cooking conditions, and sauces, and Bob agreed to be the guinea pig. After eight months, Bob and Jerry were still married, and they had a product that tested so well at the marketplace that a few fish buyers began gearing up right away for production.

Now hake isn't a fish you'll be seeing in the round. What they came up with is a frozen cake sold under the name Pacific whiting. You store it in your freezer and slice it as you need it; then broil, bake, or sauté just like any other fish. Here's Bob's favorite sauce: a little flour, lots of butter, a little cream, a little tarragon, and a touch of lemon. Mix together, pour over the fish, and bake in the oven.

Rock Cod, Sole, and Flatfish: At three dollars a pound, these are not trash fish, it is true. But these fish do have a serious problem both at the docks and on the boats. At one time or another, all of these fish find themselves being incidental to the sought-after catch.

Suppose a buyer has a market that wants five hundred pounds of sand dabs. The ocean is not an automat, so the fisherman drags his net through the water and he gets what he gets. Suppose he gets two tons of Dover sole and two hundred fifty pounds of sand dabs. The fisherman knows the buyer can't or won't handle the Dover, so he throws them back into the ocean and makes another tow—and another one—until he has five hundred pounds of sand dabs. Another problem is that even though a dragger uses a large-mesh net to allow the passage of smaller fish, once the net starts filling up with large fish, they block the holes and the small fish get caught. The buyer won't take the small fish either, because the cost of filleting so many of them for so little meat cuts into his profit—so the fisherman throws the small fish back into the water, too, and sometimes they make up half the load. The solution to the first problem is slowly forthcoming. Though these fishes often swim in mixed groups, sonars are giving the fishermen better powers to discriminate the kinds of fish under their boats. And back at the dock, flash-freeze equipment is giving the buyers better storage capacity. But the problem of small fish is still a major problem from the point of view of both food waste and the future of the fishery.

These dilemmas of incidental catch, as they are called, are by no means limited to drag fishing. In fact, if a salmon fisherman brought aboard all the dog shark, blue shark, hake, mackerel, tom cod, rock cod, and so on, that are caught along with the salmon, he'd be icing fish in his hold till three o'clock in the morning, which is the same time the alarm goes off. Not only that, but he'd come off a trip with a load of fish that probably wouldn't average two cents a pound, and he wouldn't be in business for very long. The solution here is actually quite simple. If the public started eating these good fish, I guarantee the fisherman wouldn't throw them back, nor would he care how long he spent in the ice.

Here's a recipe for candied Spanish mackerel. Cut filets of the mackerel into half-inch chunks. Soak them for three days in a solution of two parts vinegar and one part brown sugar; no baking needed, just eat like candy. This recipe can be used with any of the fish mentioned so far, though the mackerel is the tastiest.

Tuna: The problem with tuna is that people think it comes in a can. So whenever there's a problem at the cannery (and there's *always* a problem at the cannery), boats sit at the dock trying to hold their loads; sometimes this goes on for a month, and sometimes the load is lost. For the past two years the cannery price and wait have been so bad that the albacore boats have taken the situation into their own hands. They pulled together in groups of four or five boats, came into various docks from San Diego up to Eureka, printed up pamphlets showing how to fillet and cook the fish, and called the media. And from San Diego to Eureka people came and stood on the docks in long lines; they met the fishermen, saw that the tuna is actually a regulation fish with tail and fins, and tucked them under their arms for a dollar a pound. Some people loaded the trunks of their cars.

The major problem with this approach is that the week (or two) that it takes the fishermen to off-load in this manner is a very precious week. The tuna are only out there for so long, and the fishermen need to be out on the grounds catching their next load. Another problem is that the fishermen cannot touch the tuna with a knife before selling to the public without getting a dozen different licenses and as many inspections. It's simply amazing how many Californians who pride themselves on getting back to nature won't fillet a fish. Overall it won't work to have the fishermen selling directly to the public, for many reasons, but it's to be hoped that these last two years have educated thousands and thousands of people to the fact that the skin of a tuna is not made out of tin and the buyers will take it from there.

It's possible to barbecue any fish if you take care to keep it from drying out; but with albacore, California's high-grade tuna, you have a lot more flexibility on the grill because it is one of the oiliest fish in our sea. So take a filet and choose your style. My favorite is to marinate the fish for five minutes in teriyaki sauce, then throw it on the grill.

The list of underutilized species is very long; mackerel, shark, hake, herrings, croakers, tom cod, mussels . . . In fact, it is probably four or five times as long as the list of fish that are commonly found in the market. Quite clearly, the problems aren't going to be solved overnight. But here are a few suggestions that will not only help the situation but also add greatly to the pleasure and healthfulness of your meals.

One: Don't turn down something at the market because the price is too low. Amazingly, products like squid and shark didn't start selling until retailers raised their prices.

Two: Almost all seafood can be prepared in the same ways— poach it, fry it, bake it, barbecue it, and don't worry about it. The main thing to remember is that seafood cooks much more rapidly than meat. Too long in the heat and it dries out and loses flavor. Overcooked seafood is the number one source of its bad reputation.

Three: Seafood needs special protection in the freezer. Even if wrapped in aluminum foil, the meat immediately begins to lose moisture and eventually dries out and becomes "freezer burned"; it then tastes like chalk. So take an empty milk carton, put in the fish filets, fill with water, and freeze. If you have a prize fish you need to keep whole to prove that it wasn't one centimeter less than you claimed, try this method: freeze the fish; then take it out, dip it in water, and freeze for another half hour. Repeat this three or four times. This is called glazing; it seals the flavor and texture within the thin layer of ice and will hold the fish in the freezer for months.

Chapter 29

How Many Fish in the Sea?

What may seem as moot a brain twister as how many angels can sit on the head of a pin is actually a question that fisheries scientists the world over urgently need an answer to—and yesterday. It is a question that in view of the monies and minds being hurled into its vortex might better be called an obsession.

As I worked on this book, I asked people what they thought were the most important areas of research to be pursued, and even among people in fields as far apart as physical oceanography and education, one focus kept coming to the fore: populations. We need baseline population studies; we need to understand population fluctuations; we need a methodology for determining biomass. Somehow, from out of the vast expanse of human curiosity, this one question has emerged with such demand as to lord it over all the rest. First, thou shalt census the seas! And in the space of two decades the field of marine biology has aligned itself to the cause. The Inter-American Tropical Tuna Commission, for example, one of the largest world fisheries groups, has five biologists on its staff, and nineteen statisticians. Says Lloyd Ferrar, shoreside director of the research vessel the *David Starr Jordan*, "It used to be everyone coming here was from biology, and now everyone we see is from a computer modeling background."

Why this insatiable thirst for the numbers? Perhaps because human curiosity is not at the helm after all. That was a luxury for science of centuries past. As the science of life on land evolved, with questions of process, mechanism, and description slowly weaving at unfinished edges of the picture, the life of the sea was pretty much neglected. Then suddenly a hungry twentieth-century world cast a hopeful eye to the sea, just in time to watch the great fisheries of the world collapse: the anchoveta of Peru, which provided the largest volume take of any fish in the world, gone; the California sardine overnight, down from eleven thousand tons a day to nothing; the great South African anchovy fishery, collapsed. Numb shock, not curiosity, framed the question. How many fish can we take without collapsing the stock?

The 1976 Fisheries Conservation Act, the foundation of fisheries management in the United States, is based on one central concept—the MSY, maximum sustainable yield. It's a phrase that is now echoing through all the major languages of the world. How many anchovies, how many herring, how many abalones, salmon, bottomfish, tuna—how many can we take, and how many are there to begin with? And after a decade of intense study across the world seas, the only tangible result has been humiliation. We can put a man on the moon, but we can't count the fish of the seas.

Go down to your local pet store, find an aquarium full of fish, and give it a try. Count 'em! By the time you reach three you'll understand a big part of the problem. How do you know that fish number four isn't really fish number one circling around again? Out in the ocean, the schools of fish are sometimes miles across in width, moving and milling in ways that can't be seen. Even the most sophisticated sonars can't determine the shape of a large school. Even assuming you could correlate the density of a signal with the number of fish, as the sonar sweeps one dimension of the school, the rest of its galaxy is shifting inward, outward, and over itself. In addition, the greatest range on these sonars is less than a mile; in addition, a dense area of fish shadows those behind them. In conclusion, we don't even have a way to *see* the fish we're trying to count. But for the sake of argument let's assume we can, and we have completed the count and are on our way to locate the next school. How do you know that the next school isn't the same school as the first school and it beat you to the spot? OK, so you've got a very fast boat and it couldn't be. Now you have counted the second school and are looking all over creation for the third school. How do you know that third school isn't the first school and each school is like one fish in an aquarium the size of the sea? All right, assume you tagged a member of the first school with a radio beeper so you'd know the little bugger if you saw him again. Unfortunately, fish don't stay in the same school; they break up, regroup, disperse, fan out, and recoalesce, so even if you ran across the tagged fish, he might be representing the original school—and then again, he might not. Even if you had a thousand boats . . .

In 1973–74, the expanding Japanese roe market spurred sudden interest in the herring fishery on San Francisco Bay. For thousands of years, herring from the entire coast of California have come annually into the bay to spawn on its protected rocky shores. Now, suddenly there were hundreds of boats on their tails. The Department of Fish and Game needed to determine the number of fish in the bay in order to set the quota on the catch. Shouldn't be too hard. After all, the bay's just a bathtub compared to the sea. They used a variation of the egg count method, which assumes that if you can count the eggs that are laid and you know how many eggs are laid by each female, then you can determine how many fish came into the bay, a number called the spawning biomass. The first year they did this (and every year thereafter), the fishermen had a fit. In the first place, Fish and Game missed many of the spawns that occurred, which when you think about it isn't so surprising. Since these fish spawn at ten to twenty different places every year, and each year they change places, it's pretty hard to find them all in an area the size of the bay. Secondly, in making estimates of the egg count, which they did by measuring the area covered by a certain density of eggs, the Fish and Game only considered the area down to the low water mark of the tide line. "Herring spawn in deep water, too," said the fishermen, and to prove it they brought crab pot lines from ten and twenty fathoms covered with herring eggs.

"Herring only spawn at the tide line," said Fish and Game.

"No, they don't," said the fishermen.

What? Could it be? The ancient, lowly ghost of a biology question come back to haunt?

Salmon, of course, are sitting ducks for the counter. They have to come up the river to spawn, so all you have to do is stand on the bank of a narrow part of the river, or at the fish ladders at the dam, or at the mouth of the hatchery, and count them like cars going through a tollgate. In 1979, the fishermen threw another fit. Fish and Game had gotten a very low count of salmon during a drought year, and on that basis, they were going to cut out a month from the next year's salmon season. "That only proves," screamed the fishermen, "that the salmon is smarter than the scientist. Why would a fish go upstream when there's no water in there? Just because it says they have to in the biology books?" And the next year when the take of salmon was the largest it had been for twenty years, there were some mutterings about "Well, maybe the fish never did make it up to the counting stations; maybe they do sense that the streams are dry. We just don't know the biology."

CalCOFI (California Cooperative of Oceanic Fisheries Investigators) is a unique composite group from Scripps, Fish and Game, and National Marine Fisheries Service, which has as one of its objectives to tackle in a big way this problem of counting fish in the ocean. The anchovy was chosen as their main target of study because of its important position in the food chain of the California Current. What they've done is amassed a budget of four million dollars a year, enlisted the services of the research vessel *David Starr Jordan*, and overlaid the ocean with a grid pattern from Cape Mendocino to lower Baja California and out 240 miles.

To determine the biomass of anchovies, they make larval and egg tows at each of the stations outlined in black, and they do this for sixteen weeks. The cost of running the boat alone for this time is $320,000. The tow lengths and procedures are, of course, standardized, the larvae and eggs are counted for each station, and the numbers are fed into the computers back at the National Marine Fisheries Service. In 1981, when the latest survey was carried out, the anchovy spawning biomass came out to 2,803,000 short tons, plus or minus 30 percent.

In addition to the egg and larval numbers, many other factors are taken into account—the number of females that spawned, the sex ratio of the anchovy schools, the fecundity of the eggs, and so on—and still, with this heroic effort and this mountain of data, there are many people who feel that the basic assumptions are wrong, that egg mass and larval mass are not inextricably linked to biomass.

One thing that everyone concerned with this issue does agree upon is that the populations of marine organisms are prone to fluctuate wildly and unpredictably from year to year, unlike the more stable populations on land. And this, say the critics, is just one of the things that can throw the results off by factors of ten. Suppose, for example, that a predator that eats anchovy eggs is experiencing a sudden bloom. Won't the egg count then reflect more the status of the predator than that of the anchovy?

Even if the numbers were right on the nose, many experts are beginning to question this obsession with having the fish count become the heart of the fisheries management plans. Says Joe Easily, a dragger from Oregon who is currently serving on the Pacific Fisheries Management Council, "There is a basic disagreement between the fishermen and the managers that goes beyond the actual count. The managers want a fishery in which a steady, reliable amount can be harvested each year, and the fishermen don't think the resource works that way. There's no relationship between the computer models and the real world. And one problem with the computer models is that we don't have the data to set them up, and we don't have the data to put in them—in short we don't know the life histories. And the problem behind this is the problem of doing the biology of a critter you can't follow around."

And though the management scheme is quite firmly entrenched in the political structure, many fisheries scientists have come to similar conclusions. This wishful eulogy was penned by fisheries scientist Peter Larkin of the University of British Columbia:

Here lies the concept, MSY.
It advocated yields too high
And didn't spell out how to slice the pie.
We bury it with the best of wishes.
Especially on behalf of fishes.
We don't know yet what will take its place,
But we hope it's as good for the human race.

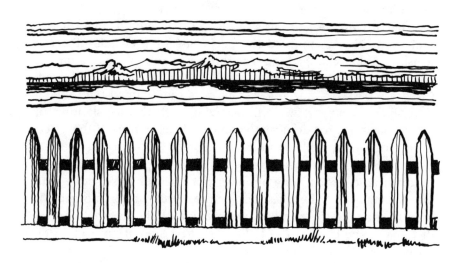

Chapter 30
Ocean Policy

Describing the current status of ocean policy in the United States doesn't make much more sense than trying to describe the shape of an amoeba. There is, however, one aspect of this issue that remains unchanging; in fact, it's a story that must have some deep significance, as it is repeated religiously in nearly every discussion of U.S. ocean policy, and then, in a tone that is usually reserved for retelling the myth of creation. "In the beginning," it goes, "President Nixon had a ferocious hate for then Secretary of the Interior Walter Hickel. So when Nixon created NOAA, he'd be damned if he'd put it in Interior where it belonged and let Walter have the dominion he was due. Instead, Nixon punished Walter by giving NOAA to the Department of Commerce where it might never be heard from again."

That's where the agreement ends. As to the effect of being stained with this original sin, some feel that ocean policy, in a department with so little clout on Capitol Hill, must forever bear the cross of impotence; others say it has made no difference at all; and other versions are somewhere in between.

One obvious reason this story is so often retold is that the formation of NOAA marked the beginning of a decade of ocean legislation that changed the seas forever from a place of anarchic wilderness to a zoned political state. In the decade that followed, Congress passed a dozen sweeping acts that framed the foundation of ocean policy. We will be living with this legislation, for better or worse, for decades to come. A brief outline of these acts is provided in the table opposite.

In their wake has been created one of the great entanglements of governance, for as one observer put it, "Congress spoke with many tongues." "The question for the 1980s," says another, "is how to manage the conflicts arising out of the internal contradictions of the laws of the 1970s. The first step of any action on the ocean is a jurisdictional dispute."

Example: The Marine Mammal Protection Act gives the National Marine Fisheries Service (NMFS) authority over porpoises, seals, sea lions, and whales. The Fish and Wildlife Service (FWS) has polar bears, walruses, sea otters, and manatees. The Endangered Species Act, covering many of the same animals, splits it up entirely differently. The agencies themselves are a broken set of twins: NMFS is in NOAA at the Department of Commerce and the FWS is at Interior.

Example: Sea turtles, while at sea, are under the jurisdiction of NMFS; while on land, they belong to the FWS.

These are only the microscopic view of what has resulted when the lead agency, NOAA, has been charged at once with protecting marine mammals, developing ocean fisheries, protecting the coastal zone, developing oil and minerals, and in general, pushing on the point of pull. The total ocean budget in 1982 was $1.2 billion, and a major portion of that was spent in the courts trying to resolve turf fights.

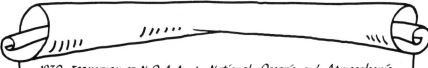

1970 FORMATION OF N.O.A.A. : National Oceanic and Atmospheric Administration.

1970 NATIONAL ENVIRONMENTAL POLICY ACT : Requires any major federal action or project be preceded by an Environmental Impact Statement and stipulates the process by which the report is produced.

1972 MARINE PROTECTION, RESEARCH & SANCTUARIES ACT : Administered by the E.P.A. Authorizes the Secretary of Commerce to designate and protect marine sanctuaries. Directs the Secretary of Commerce to determine long-range effects of pollution, over-fishing, and other activities on ocean ecosystems.

1972 COASTAL ZONE MANAGEMENT ACT : Establishes a program aimed at assisting states in developing land and water use programs for coastal zones. Administered by Secretaries of Interior and Commerce.

1972 MARINE MAMMAL PROTECTION ACT : Establishes federal responsibility for protection of marine mammals and a moratorium on the taking and importation of marine mammals. Administered by Departments of Interior and Commerce.

1973 ENDANGERED SPECIES ACT : Provides for conservation of threatened and endangered species. Authorizes agreements and grants in and for states which establish active programs for endangered species. Provides civil and criminal penalties.

1976 MAGNUSEN FISHERIES CONSERVATION AND MANAGEMENT ACT : 200 MILE LIMIT BILL. Establishes 200 mile exclusive Fisheries Economic Zone and 9 Fisheries Management Councils to establish Fisheries Management Plans in their area of jurisdiction. Sets Maximum Sustainable Yield Concept as central concept of F.M.P.'s.

1977 CLEAN WATER ACT : Provides that leasees or operators ; eg. oil companies, may be held responsible for damages due to discharges.

1978 OUTER CONTINENTAL SHELF LANDS ACT (amended) : Establishes federal jurisdiction over submerged lands on the outer continental shelf. Empowers the Secretary of Interior to grant leases. The goal of the act is to expedite development of O.C.S. minerals and oil.

1981 UNITED STATES DEEP SEA HARD MINERALS ACT : Provides that N.O.A.A. can license U.S. firms to explore and mine deposits on the deep oceans floor. The law provides that if other countries pass legislation that is similar to it ; then the U.S. would recognize the other country as a reciprocal state and would honor their licences.

Another serious complication in implementing these pieces of legislation is called the lack of science problem, which is the official way of saying nobody knows enough to carry out the mandates of the law.

Example: The Magnuson Act is far-reaching and very detailed in its plan for fisheries conservation, and the central concept is that no fish stock be harvested beyond its maximum sustainable yield. MSY is an innocuous sounding little quantum that not only depends on knowing how many fish are out there to begin with but also requires intimate knowledge of each species' reproductive cycle, its biology and ecology. The law demanded that the MSY come into use by a given date for each fish, and in one novel way or another, numbers were produced. The fishermen said, "Ridiculous," and back it went to the courts.

Example: The Outer Continental Shelf Lease Act requires that leasing decisions be based on marine productivity in the area and sensitivity of the organisms to low-level pollution. "A tall order," says Michael Glazer, a policy specialist with the Office of Coastal Zone Management, "when they're not even sure who is the predator out there and who is the prey." In this case, it's oil versus fisheries and wildlife in the courts—and NOAA is representing them all.

Dr. Biliana Cicin-Sain got her Ph.D. in urban policy during the 1970s. For a while she worked in her field. Then she got a look at the ocean policy situation and said, "Now there's a challenge!" She went to work at NOAA administration for a short time and became convinced that the decisions being made were crucial to the future of the United States, but at the same time she saw all the energy being consumed in more and more conflicts and jurisdictional disputes, with no way of resolving them. It was 1979 when she first proposed creating the Marine Policy Program at the University of California at Santa Barbara. It was her belief that the universities could help most in conflict resolution by providing a strong multidisciplinary approach and a neutral meeting ground.

Since that date, Dr. Cicin-Sain has not only brought the Marine Policy Institute into full swing, she has also organized three major conferences aimed at her initial goal of bringing people together to hash it out. One conference centered on the tricky question of U.S.–Mexican relations and the issues that revolve around the various uses of each other's waters. Another topic was the sea otter versus shellfish issue, the old marine mammal versus fisheries battle that has been in the same locked-horns position since the day the act was passed in 1972. The third conference became known to me as I began work on this section of the book. I'd ask someone a question about ocean policy, and they'd say "First you have to read the papers from the symposium on 'Future Directions in U.S. Marine Policy.'" I balked at first because I've found that many symposiums are just a series of odes to tired old cliches. But even before this conference began, Dr. Cicin-Sain's team had taken measures to ensure this wouldn't be the case. They invited people who had a lot of government experience but were not in government at the present time. It's amazing how people speak their mind when they're not afraid of losing their jobs! This symposium (reprinted in the *Marine Technological Society Journal*, 1982, 4th quarter) is the place to go for the full range of thought on the subject, should you wish to pursue it further. And that might actually turn out to be a worthwhile expenditure of energy: one unusual feature of all the federal ocean legislation is the provision for public hearings and public input at every step of decision making, much more so than in comparable legislation regarding land resources.

Ocean legislation on the state level resembles the federal, with one additional dilemma. A number of state agencies with a long history of jurisdiction on the ocean have abruptly been squeezed into a zone limited to within three miles of the shore. A significant example of this is the state Department of Fish and Game, which has regulated commercial fishing in California since the inception of the industry. With the passage of the 1976 Magnuson Act, the department was crunched behind an invisible line running up the coast and out three miles from any point of land—a complete absurdity when you consider even the most elemental observation that fish have tails propelling them from federal waters to state waters and back again faster than you can call a meeting to order. Not surprisingly, the officials with the state Department of Fish and Game are spending a great deal of their time in court. What *does* come as a surprise is that the fishermen, long the adversaries of Fish and Game, have gone to bat to help the department retain as much control as possible. "We've had a lot of disagreements over the years," says one fisherman, "and we still do. But at least they know a salmon from a shark. Most of these guys at the federal level need a map just to get to the dock."

Despite the state's weakened hand in ocean management, it is nonetheless holding a very interesting wild card. The California Coastal Act of 1976 (resulting from a 1972 voter initiative) has jurisdiction over the territory from three miles out to sea and into the shorelands anywhere from two hundred feet to five miles. It requires that local governments amend their plans to comply with the protective mandates of the California Coastal Commission. In 1972, the Federal Coastal Zone Management Act was passed. This law was engineered to encourage state governments to take responsibility for their own coastal zones. It does so by saying that if you, the state, enact programs and are able to obtain local compliance with these programs, then we, the federal government, will, one, supply money to support these programs and, two, ensure that all federal programs are consistent with your state plan.

The resounding and significant consequence of this is that the California Coastal Commission is the only state body with the power to override federal programs in the coastal zone. In January 1984, the Coastal Commission tested the strength of this law in the United States Supreme Court. Offshore oil leases can be granted for territories outside the three-mile limit, but, says the Coastal Commission, the shipping of the oil, the pipelines, and many of the other activities generated by the lease take place in and directly affect the coastal zone. Black queen on white king and check! It was a bold move when you consider that, after income taxes, oil lease sale monies are the second largest source of federal revenue. Obviously, the federal people didn't have this kind of monkey business in mind when they wrote the bill. The Supreme Court ruled against the Commission in a five-to-four decision, saying that federal offshore oil leases do not fall in the jurisdictional territory of the Coastal Commission. And although this decision does not directly attack the principle of the act, it has drastically undermined the power of the Commission.

Peter Douglas is the director of offshore energy administration in the Coastal Commission. "Once you exercise power in a way that's important," he observes, "there's the likely potential of a lot of backlash." Accordingly, the budget of the Coastal Commission has been slashed on both the federal and state level, the officially stated reason given by Governor Deukmejian—the organization is "meddlesome."

In the last few years, in fact, the whole ocean budget has been slashed below functioning levels. NOAA, in comparison to other government agencies, has had a particularly hard time holding onto its monies. It's when conversations turn to bemoaning this fate that you hear the story told again and again. "In the beginning," it goes, "Nixon had a ferocious hate . . ."

Chapter 31

The Law of the Sea Treaty

Before 1970, the ocean was little more than a mirror lightly reflecting the world of landed events; it has witnessed the passage of transport ships, its nearshore rim has supplied a little of our food, and a few of our battles have spilled into its realm. But even the first crossings of the sea derived their glory more from the lands discovered than from the crossings themselves. So far, the ocean's sheer power has kept its pristine state unshattered. Outer space, say many who have worked them both, has proved to be a less hostile environment than the sea.

The International Law of the Sea Conference of the 1970s may very well come to be seen as the opening chapter in ocean history, with world necessity being, at once, protagonist and antagonist.

For nine years during the 1970s, representatives from over a hundred nations gathered regularly to design a world ocean treaty around the philosophy of "the oceans, the common heritage of mankind." Not surprisingly, its course was touch and go. But considering the scope of the issues, the sheer area of territory in question, the conference was actually nearing the accomplishment of a miracle. The Law of the Sea Conference had forged a treaty that dealt with every present and foreseeable ocean issue of international significance.

Navigation rights through every strait on the globe were delineated; the right of innocent passage (a traditional custom of the sea) was better defined. The outer edge of the continental shelves and the breadth of the territorial seas were defined. The specifics of a world program for the prevention of marine pollution was agreed upon, as was a program for the conservation of marine mammals and programs for the management of the fishes that roam the high seas. The conduct of ocean research was prescribed, as were the conditions for seabed mining outside the 200-mile exclusive economic zones, also established by the treaty and already adopted by the countries of the world. Border settlements were defined for the tricky areas where many countries (like Japan and China, or Turkey and Greece) neighbor over a narrow band of sea. The treaty agreements also set up mechanisms of authority and conflict resolution to cover all situations imaginable to the thousands of participants in the creation of this most complex treaty ever drafted in the history of mankind.

In 1981, the job was done! The years of work had brought the vision of the Law of the Sea Treaty to reality. One more session in October to tie up loose ends and it was ready to be signed at the next meeting, to be held in spring 1982 in Jamaica. But the hope was dashed on thousands of rocks the size of an oyster. One country had found a way of extracting a pearl from every oyster, and the common heritage of mankind went the way of "Thou shalt not kill" when the Spanish missionaries discovered Incan gold.

Quite by accident, I was present at the October meeting when the tide was turned. October 1981, I was lying on a warm rock on the beach at Nanakuli, Oahu. Tropical waves rolled gently up over the rock and back into the sea again, washing away even the semblance of time. I was supposed to be putting together a fisheries education program for Hawaiian high school dropouts, but things weren't working out well at all. Cultural chasms just weren't being crossed. This alternative program, however, was working out quite well: a small group of us would meet on the beach each day around noon, take a little piece of net out on an inner tube, dive down to the bottom, tie the net to the coral, swim back to the beach, and stretch out on the rock, till hours later when someone would mention the net.

A group of Samoans came walking toward us, with the guy in the middle waving an octopus high in the air above his head. It was a really big one, and even from a distance you could tell the guy was beaming. Moki, the guy beside me, stood up to go and meet them. I stood up, too, but right away Moki's hand on my shoulder told me to sit back down. "Hey, that's the chief," he said harshly.

"Sorry, I forgot." The man with the octopus was a Samoan chief, and I had forgotten that a woman doesn't just go running up to him, especially not dressed in a pair of shorts.

I was tired of this stuff. Just then the transistor radio, even with all the sand in the speakers, managed to make an announcement about the progress of the Law of the Sea Conference being held at the Prince Kuhio hotel in Honolulu, and I thought, "A day in the real world would sure be nice."

Two hours by bus through the cane-field barrier and there I was in downtown Honolulu, America. And there was Mike from the Oceanic Society barreling up the steps of the hotel. "Hey," he said, "have you heard what's going on?"

"Sure," I said, "the Law of the Sea meeting. I needed a change of scenery."

"Oh, then you don't know," he said and started babbling about the world nickel market, manganese nodules, Elliot Richardson, an ocean mining company, and that the United States might pull the rug.

"For Christ's sake, Mike," I said, unused to the pace, "you're getter hyper. There's a nice beach fifteen minutes from here; you'd better go soak for a day." But he just kept barreling up the stairs.

Inside, recess was in full swing, and hundreds of people were milling around in the lobby. I went to the information desk to sign up and get some literature, but the lady said $250 for the conference. So I backed right up, made a full circle around the crowd, slid into the conference room, and found myself a seat—it felt good to once again exercise a little good old American ingenuity.

They resumed the meeting on the topic of tuna: discussions about rights of passage, Japanese purse seining around small island countries, proposals for setting up plants in underdeveloped nations, enforcement problems. It all seemed interesting to me, but most people were buzzing with small private conversations and obviously waiting for something else.

Noon recess and people were grouping differently, standing in tight knots, locked on each other's words, forging their thoughts like they were big iron nails needed to hold the planks on a ship. It felt too ridiculous to walk into the midst of this intensity and ask what was going on. So I went to lunch and returned a little late.

Now the conference room was packed with twice as many people, and it looked like a good third of them were reporters. I spotted a seat next to Mike, and he said, "This is it." I said, "This is what?" but a man leaning over his shoulder had already taken his attention. Then the U.S. representative was announced. Instead of speaking from the podium like the others, he walked up to a microphone in the aisle among the people. He began, "The measure of a great society is the degree of development of its technology."

I always had felt myself to be armored with more than my share of worldly cynicism, but the impact of his statement before a world body made me feel frightened. Or maybe it was the contagion from a hallful of world leaders sitting on the edge of their seats, apprehensive and overalert. Though I wasn't informed on the issue at the time, it was quite clear as the speaker went on that the United States, as Mike had said earlier, was about to pull the rug.

The general policies of the International Seabed Authority would be dictated by a plenary Assembly operating by a two-thirds majority. As a result, a majority of nations with divergent political and economic objectives, not necessarily related to seabed mining, could make decisions which would adversely affect United States access to seabed minerals. . . . The United States depends on its private companies for access to resources. The Draft Convention would create an unfavorable climate for private investment in seabed mining. Indeed, if seabed mining were to take place under the treaty, it is possible that in order to compete, private companies in the U.S. might decide to operate joint ventures. As a result, the U.S. could remain dependent on foreign sources of supply for certain strategic minerals.

Indeed, a treaty that would create such serious obstacles to direct national access to seabed minerals would not likely obtain the advice and consent of the U.S. Senate. . . .

At the conclusion, the chairman asked for comments, and one by one, people from all over the world got up and tried to find the words to diplomatically register their despair and disappointment. Mostly they talked about the history of the treaty and all the years of work. A striking-looking man stood up with his hastily scribbled notes. He was an ambassador from Indonesia. "Listen to this guy," said Mike. "He's sharp." I tried, but I couldn't concentrate on his words; I just saw his hands trembling trying to restrain the emotion.

In the spring of 1982, the United States refused to sign the treaty. Israel, Turkey, and Venezuela were the only other nations that refused to sign. Some say the treaty has been irreparably weakened. Others say that it is the United States that has been weakened. The ocean is an awfully big place to be on your own.

Across the vast sweep of issues covered by the treaty, the majority of the stipulations were favorable to the United States. But during the latter part of the negotiations, U.S. consortiums had found a way to mine the rich deposits of manganese nodules from the deep ocean floor. The treaty stipulated that if a country wanted to lease an area of seabed for mining, it had to give up the income of a comparable area to the Seabed Authority as designated in the treaty, with this income to be shared by landlocked and third world nations—a strategy commensurate with the concept of the oceans as the common heritage of mankind. The treaty also stipulates that in regard to ocean mining on the seabed, the developed countries had to share the technical know-how with the third world.

"It's depressing," said Mike when I talked with him three years later. "It's depressing that we didn't sign ten years of world effort because we don't want to share our technology. It's also an interesting recent development that the whole thing may have turned out to be a moot question. The thing now is that no bank will put up that kind of money for seabed mining without the security of an international agreement. Not only that, but it looks like the manganese nodules may be out of date. Deposits of polymetallic sulfides have been found on the ocean floor that contain the same precious minerals, and not only are they in much shallower water, they are also lying within our own 200-mile exclusive economic zone, where the treaty has no authority."

According to Dr. Cicin-Sain at the Marine Policy Institute at the University of California at Santa Barbara, "The developing world sees it as a real breach of faith by the United States after working hard for so many years on a treaty. Now the United States is having to try to develop bilateral treaties with each individual country, and these countries are saying, 'We don't want bilateral treaties. We already spent a lot of years together saying what we want.'"

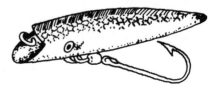

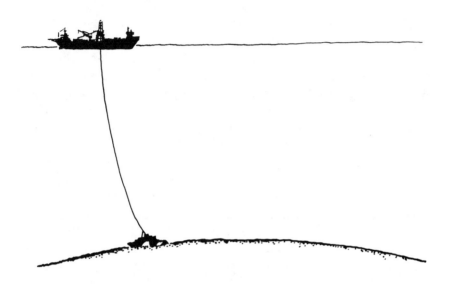

Chapter 32

The Ocean Mining Company

Manganese nodules were discovered over a hundred years ago by one of the first oceanographic research vessels, the HMS *Challenger*, but they remained a scientific curiosity until the early 1960s. It was in the recent upsurge of ocean science that more and more of these nodules were found on the ocean floor, and it was the current world climate of mineral depletion that endowed the manganese nodules with the aura and authority of gold. Manganese nodules contain manganese, nickel, copper, and cobalt — four minerals that are as vital to modern society as amino acids are to life.

In the late 1960s Lockheed Aircraft wanted to diversify, and they decided to see how they could use advanced military technology in the oceans. In 1977, they formed the Ocean Mining Company, a consortium of Lockheed, Standard Oil Indiana, Royal Dutch Shell, and Royal Bos Kalis. They had one objective: to research and develop the mining of manganese nodules, to mine the product and sell it.

Conrad Welland was chosen to head the project. His first career was in the Navy as an aviator and electronics specialist developing radar, sonar, missiles, and weapons systems associated with the oceans. After retiring from the Navy, he went to Lockheed, where he did research work in the space program; when the Ocean Mining Company was formed, he joined them.

The following are some of Conrad Welland's views on ocean mining, the Law of the Sea Treaty, and the future of both.

"We [Ocean Mining Company] have spent, to date, one hundred thirty million just on the research and development, exploration, and equipment testing. We know now that if we find any mineral deposits on the seafloor, we can get them. The technology of mining is not the problem. Depth is not a problem. We've put tons of heavy machinery on the ocean floor, machinery with thousands of horse power, hydraulic and electrical machinery, down to fifteen thousand feet, and at fifteen thousand feet we have excellent control over this machinery. That's not the problem; we can recover the minerals.

"But we've put the whole thing on the back burner. Right now we're cut back to an office and a secretary and a few employees. In the last few years two things have happened that caused us to put our operations on hold. The first is that the Law of the Sea activity made political and legal problems much greater than we had thought. Originally we thought the LOS would be a good thing; we thought we'd be operating under the freedom of the seas. But the third world decided that they would make a big political thing out of it, because they have what they call the New International Economic Order, which says that the reasons the developed countries are so wealthy and the developing countries are so poor is because we took all the wealth away from them. Of course, this is strictly a political thing and completely wrong, and it won't solve any of their problems. We didn't take their wealth away from them. Wealth is created; it's created by big investments in research and development and knowledge and capability. That's the way you develop wealth.

"You see, the way the LOS is set up in regard to ocean mining is this. The treaty would establish a Seabed Authority, which would be composed of all the people that signed the treaty. The Seabed Authority would establish the enterprise, which would get money from the people who signed the treaty. It's the enterprise that would do the mining; the Seabed Authority would be like a U.N. of the sea, if you want to call it that, and 25 percent of the money would come from the United States. The treaty also has in it a forced transfer of technology. If we were to work under the Seabed Authority, we'd have to transfer all our technology and knowledge to the Seabed Authority and to all the countries who are members. We're willing to transfer technology, but it has to be a situation in which both sides are going to benefit. It'll never happen until then. People don't understand this. The third world is saying, you give us the money and we will go ahead and develop it. Well, they're incapable of doing it, and who's going to risk that kind of money with a group that doesn't know how to operate?

"I was heavily involved on the LOS as an advisor to the State Department. I attended all the meetings in New York and Geneva. I'm chairman of the Interseas Mineral Resources Committee, and I'm a member of the executive committee for the LOS Institute in Hawaii. I just got back from there three weeks ago on this particular issue of the third world. I know these people well, though we're on totally opposite sides of the street. I keep telling them that what they're doing is counterproductive for their own future.

"I feel it was a very important thing that the Reagan administration decided not to sign the treaty, and I think this will be borne out despite conversations among what I call 'one worlders' or the liberal establishment. They don't understand the problems of trying to work under the treaty. That one hundred thirty million we spent was just the entry fee into this business; from there, it will take ten years and one and a half to two billion dollars' investment before we get a dollar back on the manganese nodules. And all that money is coming from our partnership—it's all privately invested money. Under the Seabed Authority, the United States would be supplying 25 percent of the financing, and the technology and profits would be spread over the world.

"One hundred twenty-seven out of one hundred sixty-seven have signed the treaty, but to date, only six or seven nations have ratified it, and none of the communist or developed nations is among them. Many, many treaties are signed, but until they're ratified, they're ineffective. The League of Nations is an example; we signed it, but we didn't ratify it. The fact that the United States didn't even sign has had a big effect on other nations, because, as I said, the United States would have been a 25 percent contributor.

"There are six consortia worldwide that have gotten into this ocean mining and every one of them has spent a lot of money. A French consortium owned by the French government, a Japanese consortium owned by the Japanese government, a Canadian group, and three groups in the United States, all three of them privately owned like Ocean Mining Company. We have all settled the differences among ourselves; we've adjusted our claims to the seabed so there's no overlap problem. We're not worried about a gold-rush situation, because of the amount of money and capital it takes to get into the game.

"In 1981, the United States passed the Deep Sea Hard Minerals Act. This act says that NOAA can license U.S. firms to explore and mine deposits in the deep oceans and provide for the required environmental controls. The law also provides that if other countries pass legislation that is similar to ours, then the United States would recognize that other country as a reciprocal state and would honor their licensees. The United States, Japan, England, Germany, Italy, the Netherlands, and Belgium have come to such an agreement. And right now we are awaiting our license to mine between Hawaii and Mexico. This act has solved our legal political problems. It took us nine years to get it through. It was set up in anticipation of problems with the LOS.

"The main reason we're on hold now is because world metals have been expanded, and it may be another five years before the market is ripe. In the meantime other mineral possibilities are opening up—the polymetallic sulfides off the Gorda Ridge right here in California, for example, and the manganese crusts on top of sea mounts. At present they need further study. But there's no doubt in my mind that we'll find other deposits out there worth mining. There's so much area out there, and we're improving our exploration tools every day."

Chapter 33

The Cop on the Corner

From reading the newspapers, the public thinks there is a direct connection between sewage and tumors or lesions in fish. We think there may be another explanation.

We think the outfall might create a greater food supply for certain kinds of fishes, and that therefore, there would be less competition when it comes time to eat. In other words, a fish wouldn't have to work so hard for his supper.

And this led us to think that maybe a fish with a tumor or a lesion or some other affliction might consider himself lucky, if he didn't have to fish to eat. So, he and other weakened fishes would

be attracted to the outfall, where they are caught by persons moni-
toring the area.

Ted Dunn, former chief of laboratory operations
for the Orange County Sanitation Districts

There isn't an activity, project, or predicament on the ocean that
isn't covered by the most up-to-date environmental legislation.
Every fishery has a sophisticated, inch-thick management plan.
Every lease sale is accompanied by lengthy provisos and strictly
defined parameters limiting the ecological impact of the operation,
and so too mining, drilling, and the discharge of materials at sea.
The intent of the surge of ocean legislation of the 1970s was to
protect the sea. The legislation, however, neglected to account for
one little facet of human nature—out of sight, out of mind. Compliance was left to wishful thinking.

A warden or inspector on land costs a salary and maybe a jeep.
To put the same person on even the nearshore areas of the sea
costs $50,000 for the boat, $60,000 to $100,000 for the captain and
the crew, and a minimum of $15,000 a year maintenance. Off-
shore, the costs are greatly multiplied. This is just one reason that
ocean enforcement exists in the intent of the legislation, in the
headlines of the newspapers, and in the minds of the beholders,
but not on the ocean itself.

Jim Steel works for the Department of Fish and Game. He's
head of the water quality division, covering the territory from San
Diego to San Luis Obispo. He is responsible for monitoring all oil
activities in the area for pollution, and for checking all discharge
into the sea from outfalls, as well as nonpoint sources and all
other runoffs. He has 1.2 billion gallons of sewage a day running
into his territory and 7 billion gallons of hot water from the power
plants. "I have a pretty good lab," he says, "but I don't have any
staff to run it, and I have a 1973 Plymouth."

The amazing thing about Jim, however, is his unfailing, high-
spirited humor. I read him the quote that begins this section,
expecting an outraged reaction, but instead he just laughed. "I've
heard a lot of bullshit in this job, but that's good, that's really very
good." Why would such a fun-loving guy take the job of stem-
ming the tide of bullshit and shit run amok? "I wanted to save the

world, like everyone else, so I went to work for Fish and Game. My job, at first, was to study endangered species. I was studying the habitat of this endangered snake for some time, when one morning I went to work and the bulldozers were there ahead of me. I wondered how something like this could have happened. So I got into this end of the work, environmental advocacy, and now I know how it happens.

"Those that want a release from secondary [sewage] treatment requirements have all kinds of arguments. The one you gave me is pretty good, but usually they argue that the biomass is higher near the outfalls. And this is true, the sewage by itself can be considered a food source. But what happens if the pollution is there for any length of time, one organism outcompetes the others and the species diversity goes down. And it's the lower organisms that win out. *Capitella capitata* is a worm you can find at any polluted outfall in the world. It's the standard; it does the best and proliferates in tremendous numbers, so the overall biomass stays the same. But it's like killing a 300-pound cow and getting 300 pounds of maggots and arguing that you didn't change the biomass. Who wants the whole world to be for the flies?

"The sewage has really affected the fisheries in southern California. The Santa Monica Bay used to have a lot of kelp and a lot of sport fish right out on the bay, and now there's nothing but a few sick fish. The high pollution levels used up all their vitamins because of the stress, and that's why they're full of lesions. But even the substrate of the area has been affected. It used to be a harder substrate, and now it's a much softer mud that supports a lower diversity of animals and has a lower productivity. There's no doubt that this is a consequence of all the activity landside, but how much is due to the siltation or to street pollution or to the outfalls is hard to say; no one can really say. Especially not me, I can't even work my lab. There's a group called the Southern California Water Research Project. Ask me who funds this project." Jim wanted to be sure I didn't miss the subtleties. "It's funded by the water dischargers," he said. "They have a half million dollars, and they do all the science, and when it comes time to do battle I have nothing. Now they've taken the outfalls and moved them farther out to sea, out beyond the area of user interest, outside of their visibility. But it's still the same sewage creating the same problems. They've also taken to removing the particulate matter from the sewage before discharge into the sea, which is very effective in removing a lot of the sins and looks very good in print. The only trouble is that they're taking the sludge and putting it in a different outfall, so it's still going into the sea. They're always one step ahead.

"And with all the activity down in southern California, I'm the *only* guy in Fish and Game for Marine Water Quality Control. The water quality control boards of each district have some overlap in jurisdiction to be sure, but they're worried about all benefits, which not only include my interests but what they call human interests as well. In other words, they're interested that the sewage get dumped. Besides, they don't have anyone on their staff to determine if there's a biological problem with the sewage in the ocean. There's no one looking at it from the standpoint of the environment—that's my job and I'm outnumbered. That's why arguments like the one you read me carry so much weight.

"Oil pollution is my job too. Contrary to what most people think, oil floating on the surface of the ocean is not the main problem. The insidious part of oil pollution is the total hydrocarbon levels dissolved in the water column. It changes the whole ocean in our little corner of the world to such an extent that the competitive balance among the animals is changed. Most of this oil gets in the water through sewage outfalls. What happens is when they drill to the level of the oil, they frequently also drill through a freshwater aquifer, and that allows the oil to commingle with the water. When they take this mixture back to the refinery, they put it through separators and, of course, they keep the oil, and you know where the water goes, right back into the ocean. But it still has high levels of dissolved hydrocarbons. From time to time the hydrocarbon levels in our area get so high from this and other sources that people can taste them in the fish.

"Compliance with the laws is our biggest problem. The Environmental Protection Agency has finally started to ask me what we need, but that's taken years. I tell them we need a cop on the corner.

"But the EPA wants to take all the arguments and make them

generic in nature. What they did with the bad drilling muds is a good example. They made a study of a few platforms and based their evaluation of all platforms on those few. And I said, 'No way, that's merely the demonstration study method that's been used in too many other situations, and it's never caught anyone doing anything wrong.' What I want is a characterization of each area of discharge—what's going to be in the discharge, the fish that are going to be affected—and I want somebody out there making damn sure that whatever standards are set are in fact being met by the people on the platform. One problem we have with that right now is that the guys on the platform have total control over who comes on the platform and when.

"But EPA hasn't even been going out to look, they decry manpower. They assume because the laws are written down that there's compliance. Just before the last big hearing, EPA did finally send a guy out there to all the platforms real quick just to say they've been out there. But that doesn't do it. For one thing, I know the guy, and he doesn't have a clue about what to look for. There's quite a science involved in being able to see what's going on. And for another thing, he didn't even take any drill mud samples to send into the lab. It's all a ruse.

"The oil companies at the management level keep telling me that they're very concerned, that they want to do things correctly, that they want to play ball. And I say, 'That's great, why don't you come with me and we'll go out to a platform and I'll show you right now that they're not playing ball.' But then the mood changes, and of course, management says it doesn't want to interfere with production. They say they want us to be the cop on the corner; they say the laws are on our books; and, of course, they know full well that we don't have any teeth.

"We don't have any teeth, we don't have any manpower, and we don't have any money. And it just doesn't make any sense. The paradox is that everyone I talk to is so concerned, and yet it never gets backed up with money for pollution monitoring and detection. Right now, there is no cop on the corner. If we had a good strong team with solid money, these folks would know that they'd get caught if they did something wrong. But the way it is now, why should they comply?"

Chapter 34

Mussel Watch

In the late 1960s, the pelican was suffering severe losses of its young. The shells around their eggs were so thin and fragile they crumbled before the embryos had fully developed. At the same time sea lions were being observed to have very high rates of premature births and stillborn calves. Studies showed massive concentrations of DDT in both animals, but as always, this new information posed more questions than it answered: Is this DDT the cause? Is it coming from the water? Is the level increasing? How can we measure it? This last question was the stickler, because concentrations in the water were so low as to be unmeasurable, and obviously you couldn't go hunting down a sea lion or a pelican every time you wanted to take a measurement.

In 1976, Dr. Ed Goldberg, a marine chemist at Scripps, drove around the country collecting mussels from harbors, bays, and open coast on a grant from the Environmental Protection Agency. This was his group's ingenious answer to the problem of measuring pollutants in the marine environment. The mussel is a common bivalve the world over; it is a filter feeder, pulling tremendous volumes of water through its system in a short time. Most appealing of all, mussels are easy to "catch." You simply walk out at low tide and pluck them from a rock. And you can go back to the same spot time and time again. Dr. Goldberg shipped mussels from each location back to Scripps, where they were tested for metals, petroleum products, synthetic organics (like DDT), and radioactive materials. This was the beginning of Mussel Watch, a program for monitoring pollutants in the sea, which is presently being expanded throughout the world.

For the first three years, the objective was to construct a data base to determine a baseline so that future measurements in the area would give an accurate indication of change. Even so, some interesting results emerged early in the game. The waters around Los Angeles, in fact, the waters of the whole Southern California Bight, including the southern islands, produced mussels that were hot with DDT. Looking at the profiles of the concentrations, the residues were traceable to the White Point outfall of Los Angeles. This finding was suspicious, because back in 1971 a plant called Montrose Chemical had been shut down for dumping nineteen metric tons of DDT in the water, and there didn't seem to be any reason for the current high levels. Nonetheless, Mussel Watch alerted EPA and the Water Quality Control Board, and the pursuant investigation found that fresh DDT was indeed still being released at this site and was part of the Montrose legacy. Seventy thousand pounds of the stuff was still clinging to the pipes of the outfall, and an undetermined amount was slowly being leached in runoff from the land dumps used by Montrose after they were forced to abandon direct release into the water system. The theory has been that DDT would eventually settle to the bottom and be buried in the sediment. But according to Jim Little of the Department of Fish and Game, there are still one hundred tons of DDT floating around in the San Pedro Basin, and in accord with the results of Mussel Watch, they're even finding this stuff in the sand animals on the beach.

Another interesting result of Mussel Watch came out of the large, tasty mussels that thrive in the waters of the Farallon–Point Reyes area. They contained plutonium isotopes in barely detectable amounts. But the ratio of these isotopes was identical to the ratio of plutonium isotopes produced by the above-ground atomic testing conducted in the Pacific years before. The group is following this lead, in the belief that mussels may be an excellent organism for monitoring atomic testing around the world. Even more provocative was their finding that the levels of these compounds increased markedly after periods of intense upwelling. Once pulled out of the inanimate mass of earth into the tightly bounded web of life in the sea, these poisons do not easily, if ever, get out. A fish eats the mussel, the sea lion eats the fish, the sea lion dies and sinks to the bottom. There, attended by trillions of bacteria in the black, unknown depths, it decays into the amorphous muck of the seemingly most eternal burial place on earth. But spring arrives, the upwellings fountain the nutrient debris from the sea floor, the planktons bloom, and the progeny of the dead animals are nourished—with the poisons that won't go away.

Dr. Bob Riseborough is currently heading the second phase of Mussel Watch. Strangely enough, he got into the program through an employment agency. He had completed his graduate work in biology and wanted to travel. But first he needed some money. A quick, short-term job, he thought, and headed down to the employment office, where the University of California had just posted a request for someone to case the docks and collect specimens from the fishermen. The group was connected to Mussel Watch, and since then Dr. Riseborough has been traveling more than he could have dreamed. He picks up languages as easily as passports and has been organizing conferences of scientists and government officials throughout the world to assist them in establishing their own Mussel Watch programs. Currently, the Regional Seas Program of the United Nations Environmental Program is proposing to use a version of Mussel Watch in a global monitoring scheme. And West Pack (a group of Western Pacific Nations) has started a similar program.

The ingenious concept of using mussels to monitor pollution was indeed a breakthrough, in light of the tremendous technical difficulties inherent in measuring compounds so diluted by the sea. But perhaps, in the long run, it is the international thrust of the Mussel Watch program that carries the most significance, since any project on the sea that ignores the global perspective of one world ocean lacks a link to the future.

Chapter 35

Margaret Owings

"Great things begin in the tiny seed of the small change in the troubled individual heart. One single, lonely, inexperienced heart has to change first — and all the rest will follow."

These are words from the writings of Laurens van der Post. They were spoken by Rachel Carson when she received the National Audubon Society award medal. Twenty years later, just prior to her death, Rachel Carson wrote a note to Margaret Owings asking her to repeat the line, which she did at her own acceptance of the same award. Margaret Owings lives in California at her home in Big Sur. And if you don't recognize her name, you are certain to recognize the name of her organization, the Friends of the Sea Otter, a forceful example of what can follow from the tiny seed of a small change in the individual heart.

I first heard of Margaret Owings while fishing just outside the kelp beds at Fort Ross. Another fisherman spotted a sea otter in the kelp, which was a big deal because it was the first time he had seen a sea otter there since he was a kid. It was also a big deal because this was back in the early 1970s before the fishermen and the environmentalists had figured out that they were hitched to the same cart. But what really made this a full-charge event was the fact that there weren't many fish that day, and as is usual under those conditions, all hands were on their radios, looking for a good topic to grind through the improvisational mill. This poor sea otter was it. And the first question that came up was, how many friends do you figure there are for each sea otter in California? Another fisherman came over the radio immediately with an answer. "I don't know how many," he said, "but the way you find out is count the number of times Margaret Owings opens her mouth, multiply by ten, and divide by the number of sea otters."

"Who's Margaret Owings?" I interrupted.

The response that came back was given seriously: "She's the mastermind of environmental organization in the state of California."

No doubt Margaret Owings has been paid more poetic tribute, but nonetheless, this impressed me enough to contact her ten years later and ask her about her life and work. Now, you're probably thinking, as I was, that it takes a lot of experience and grooming before you can voice your concerns and activate your ideas through a powerful organization; but take heart and hope, and take notice from the life of Margaret Owings. She was in her forties before she even began.

"I was raised in Carmel and I used to walk around Point Lobos as a young girl. That's when I discovered the sea gardens and tide pools. But I didn't become involved with wildlife preservation until I had already lived part of my life in Chicago, returned to California, and started my life again in Big Sur.

"One day a truck fired at a sea lion that lived on the beach. I heard the shot and saw that he killed it. I ran as fast as I could up to the highway, but the truck had already left. When I got back to the house, I was so infuriated that I wrote a letter to the *Monterey Herald* and ended it by saying that the man 'had taken a life greater than his own.' I got a lot of mail, some of it good and some of it mockery. But I saw what a letter could do.

"Not long after, in 1959, the state senate had put up a bill proposing to kill off 75 percent of the sea lions on the coast because they were eating some of the salmon on the Klamath River. The plan entailed blasting the beaches, poisoning the waters, and using explosives. And no one was awake to what was going to be done. I'd never done anything like this before, but I began getting some scientific information from Scripps, working with a lobbyist, talking and writing to the press, and getting people to write letters. We got so many letters to the legislators that we defeated the bill. Then the senator who first introduced the bill heard there was a woman south of Carmel who was making all the fuss, and he also heard that she had sea lions below her house. That same year he introduced a new bill that said that the area just below my house would be a reserve for sea lions. That made me so mad that we defeated that one too.

"That's how it began. I wasn't connected to conservation groups, and I had never even been up to the legislature. And many of the things that we can do easily now, like make a photocopy or get a TV short, were almost impossible then."

Using this experience as her starting block, Margaret proceeded to stop the bounty hunting on the mountain lion in California. It was such an impressive success that she was appointed state park commissioner, where she says she learned her way around Sacramento. And then one day the Natural Resources Committee of the state senate was called down to San Luis Obispo to a meeting with the abalone fishermen. One of the senators said casually to Margaret, "Why don't you come along?" One wonders if he was aware that he was putting fire to the wick of a very luminous and enduring light.

"Everyone who was there at the meeting, except for myself, was saying death to the otter. They wanted to kill all the sea otters because they were coming south and eating the red abalone. I listened and thought about it all the way home.

"And I wrote another letter to the *Monterey Herald;* this one I ended by saying that the sea otter needs a friend. The editor boxed the letter on the front page and gave it the heading 'Who's going to start the Friends of the Sea Otter!' When I saw that, I knew it had to be me; I knew I had to answer my own letter." Which she did, and today, Friends of the Sea Otter numbers over six thousand members and has been instrumental in obtaining many of the local and national mammal protection bills of the last decade, including the Marine Mammal Protection Act and the Endangered Species Act. And today, Margaret Owings is one of the most knowledgeable conservationists and most powerful spokespersons for our coastal ecology.

How did all this happen? As might be expected, Margaret wanted most to talk about the current struggles with the oil companies and the attempts to replant the otter on the southern islands, but she did take a few moments to look back over the process itself. "I think one thing that is very interesting is that one individual, working as a solitary person, can often be more effective. You can let the movement grow later, but especially in the beginning, without the hindrance and arguments of a committee, one person can just push and push on a straight line without distraction. Another thing is that you have to narrow yourself down. Of course I care about the grizzly bear and the wolves in Texas, but I have to know the limits of my energy. You can't let yourself get overwhelmed by the immensity of the problems. Certainly, one could hurl oneself down and scream, but you just have to keep going."

About the personal qualities that Margaret brings to her monumental campaign, Carol Fulton, one of her long-time co-workers, spoke without hesitation: "Margaret is an artist with words, one of her favorite books is the thesaurus. She takes great pains to find the perfect word to get an idea across. And she's not afraid to use emotional words. This is how she is able to quicken the public's awareness, to bring things to life for people who perhaps have never experienced them. At the same time, she is meticulous in basing her arguments on sound scientific information. She keeps right on top of the research. In this, and in everything she does, she expects the highest degree of excellence in herself. And even in these days of watching the hard-won national commitment to conservation being trashed, Margaret remains tireless and warm. These backward times have been a great heartache after all these years, but she continues automatically. She is indefatigable."

Chapter 36

Onward Through the Fog

If someone were to gather all the necessary facts and figures, it wouldn't surprise me at all if our most valuable harvest from the sea turned out to be the data itself. Granting and regulatory agencies spend millions and millions for this stuff every year. And if not the most valuable in terms of dollars, it is certainly the most critical, for out of this data we process the decisions that determine our future course at sea. But all of this knowledge can be a dangerous illusion—you catch a fish from the sea and it is always a fish, but the data is not always the truth.

Start with a brief look at the process. In 1970 the National Environmental Policy Act (NEPA) was passed, which required that the environmental impact statement (EIS) be a weighing arm for decision making on any new project that might affect the environment. It requires that a related government agency be put in charge of preparing this statement through a process clearly defined by the law. It begins with "scoping," a new word in the English language; it is a process for determining what issues to address in the EIS, drawing on input from groups, individuals, and agencies who have something to say on the subject. The draft environmental impact statement (DEIS) is written from this material and then distributed to the scopees and the general public. This is usually followed by public hearings, which are then followed by publication of the final environmental impact statement. The final EIS must deal with and answer the issues raised at the public hearing.

In a burst of diligence, I took a day and read one of these, the DEIS for oil lease sale number 73. This regards the Department of the Interior proposal to lease two million acres, three to sixty miles out, off the coast between Point Conception and Morro Bay. This area represents prime fisheries territory in central California, and as such, it is a hotly contested package. The report is about the size of the Sacramento telephone book, and it reads about as well. But the work that obviously went into this report is phenomenal, a demonstration of high-tech communication amassing vast amounts of information on every available aspect of science, sociology, economics, law, and industry pertaining to the lease area. You have to leaf through one of these volumes yourself to truly appreciate the detail and depth.

But for present purposes consider the map, a wall-sized poster, a professional, full-color map entitled Commercial Fisheries folded into the frontispiece of the report. Through the use of a grid overlaid on the water and a color code, this map summarizes at a glance the areas of most intense fish production along the coast; the type of fish is indicated with a number code, also placed in the grid. Data on the tonnage and location of catch for twenty-six commercially important species has been accumulated and arranged with such careful attention and artistry that in a second I can tell you, for example, that in 1977 over one million pounds of salmon were caught in the block right in front of Fort Bragg, the block in front of Point Arena, and the block in front of Bodega Bay. Special attention was given to this data, of course, because it is central to the question at hand.

Now, step down to the commercial fish dock for a minute, and see how this data has been gathered for the last forty years. It doesn't matter which port, for from Crescent City to San Diego the same effortless sleight of hand occurs perhaps thirty times a day, an innocent twist of fate that unhinges the mountain of work. A fisherman pulls up to unload, the dock crew assembles, the captain stands by the scales while his crew throws fish from the hold into the bins on the end of the hoist; the buyer looks up and sees three or four more boats waiting on the outside, burns a little rubber on the forklift, rustles through the papers on his desk, pulls out the Fish and Game book and fills in the species, weight, price, and block number, hands a copy to the fisherman, puts a copy on his desk, and later on sends a copy to the Fish and Game. The block number is the number that indicates where the fisherman caught his fish! In eight years of fishing, I never once had a buyer ask me, or heard him ask anyone else, where we caught the fish. He knows better! In part it's a matter of manners, in the same way you don't ask the supplier of your business where he made his money for the day. But, in addition, the buyer is the last person you want to tell, because he'll naturally tell all his other fishermen, and the spot of fish that took you two days running around the ocean to find will quickly be a dry hole loaded with boats. If he did ask a fisherman where he got his fish, ninety-nine times out of a hundred the fisherman would give the customary "I got them a little southwest of here," which, of course, only happens to encompass a few million square miles.

So the buyer does what he's been doing ever since these tags came out forty years ago. He writes down the same number all the time, a pet number, a number he's memorized for a particular spot at sea; or like most every other buyer on the coast, he writes down the block number that corresponds to the location of his buying station. That's why the impact report shows such an overwhelmingly abundant catch of so many different kinds of fish right in front of the fish companies' doors for every fishing port on the coast. The information is dead wrong for every fish in every case. I can comment on the salmon because I was there in 1977, and I know that most of these fish came from Cape Mendocino and Point Reyes, areas on the chart that show next to nothing. The area of the proposed lease also shows a sparse catch, and this is because most of the many kinds of fish caught in the lease area are delivered to Santa Barbara, Morro Bay, or Moss Landing. All the work, the money, the data processing, all the trust being put into this chart is a total joke—but, unfortunately, it could be a dangerous joke.

What is perhaps even more distressing is that anyone looking at this chart, really looking at it, whether they be a fisheries specialist, a farmer in Iowa, or a secretary in an office in Washington, D.C., could tell that the information is contrary to common sense. A fish doesn't inhabit alternating squares on the ocean with big blank spaces in between. It's obvious that, of all the people who handled this data, *nobody* really looked at what it means. The concern was with producing data, not truth. The Department of Fish and Game has known from day one how the fish buyers write up the tags—they have wardens standing right there on the dock. But as long as there's a number placed in the box, the product is salable. And the granting and regulatory agencies can show taxpayers results for their dollars.

This is neither an isolated case nor an insignificant one. In fact, this particular data derived from the fish tags is used again and again. Another example: in 1981, the Navy announced its intent to dump nuclear submarines in the oceans. The Navy contracted Sandia National Laboratories to prepare the DEIS. Two sites were to be chosen for the dumping, one on the East Coast and one on the West Coast. They were to be deeper than two thousand fathoms, away from human activity, away from fishing and strong currents, and within the 200-mile exclusive economic zone (EEZ). Cape Hatteras was chosen on the East Coast—it's a great fishing ground and in the fastest currents in the whole North Atlantic. On the West Coast they chose a block 185 miles due west of Cape Mendocino. Nothing doing out there, says the data, even as albacore swim across the surface in schools that sometimes reach from horizon to horizon, as far as the eye can see.

Chapter 37

The Dolphin and the Tunamen

The American dream still has electricity in San Diego; the city is populated with believers. Thousands of people for whom the dream has become reality move here from all over the country, and as many thousands more come here from Mexico with the dream right on the tips of their tongues. You can see them promenading the streets at night, especially down at the wharf, under the bright lights, among the classy restaurants, and in view of the magnificent old sailing ships restored with the fanciest coil of the ropes and the highest gloss in the paint. And tied right in there, too, is the city's mirror image on the sea. The American tuna fleet —modern, clean, and sleek. Two-million-dollar vessels up to three hundred feet long, with helicopter pads atop the bridge, mile-long nets stacked in the stern, hydraulic power blocks on the boom, and deck lights brighter than the street lights. These are America's finest fishing boats; they can travel the world for months at a time and return with up to two thousand tons of refrigerated tuna in the holds.

On one of them, a deckhand was scrubbing away under brilliant floodlights on an already spotless deck. "Are they bitin'?" I asked, fully confident that a few minutes of fish talk would get me an invite to see the boat. He couldn't show me around personally, he said, because nothing but an abandon-ship order will get you out of scrub duty, but the deckboss was aboard and would be happy to take me around. We walked along the inside companionway, and the first thing we came to, right in the heart of the ship, was a small chapel to the Virgin Mary. The deckhand crossed himself and headed me into the galley. He was introducing me to Carlo, but I couldn't keep my eyes from scanning the room. I've seen a lot of fishboat galleys, and this wasn't one of them. It looked more like the entertainment suite on the "Love Boat," with great long tables, overhead TVs, and a bar with any kind of drink I wanted. And the deckhand had already gone back to his work before I realized that Carlo couldn't speak twenty words of English.

I found out later that he'd been in this country working on the tuna boats for twenty-seven years, and he just never had cause to learn English. Not that Carlo was unwilling to learn a second language; it was just that, aside from his native Portuguese, the only other language he needed to know was Spanish, international language of tunamen. And I said, "Well, if you're willing to talk slower than you ever talked in your life, then I can understand you." He said, "I don't care," and I knew he didn't. He was obviously in that mood of a fisherman who was getting panicked by the land and needed very much to kill the time before heading back to sea.

The last trip had been sour. In three months they had traveled over ninety thousand miles, crossed the international date line nineteen times, and ended up with less than five hundred tons of tuna, how much less he didn't want to say. The problem was the water over at Guam; it was so clear that the fish dove before they could close the set.

"Maybe we're the lucky ones," he said, with a sudden change of mood. "The *Regina* had a deeper net and they came in with fifteen hundred ton, and they're still over at the cannery pumping on their refrigeration, waiting for a chance to unload. You see, after the last cannery strike a couple of years ago, Bumblebee packed up and went to Samoa, and the port of San Diego is now a one-cannery town. And when my buddy Vince came in to unload, the cannery told him they couldn't handle the volume and he'd have to wait sixty days to unload. You know what Vince said then? He pointed to a big fillet knife on the table where they were talking and he said, 'Why don't you slit my throat instead?'"

Suddenly Carlo stood up, raising his drink to the moment. "Tomorrow," he said, as if issuing a mischievous command to fate, "right after we put the deeper net on the boat, we sail for New Zealand where luck will come our way. You want to see the rest of the boat?"

Staterooms the size of your living room, wall-to-wall carpeting, individual showers, and up on the bridge it looked like mission control—satellite navigation systems; Comsat, a new system for telephoning anywhere in the world; and a special radar just to keep track of the helicopter. "Nowadays," he said, "if we see birds on the horizon, we send the helicopter over to take a look."

"What about the —" and for the hundredth time that night I was stopped by the lack of a single word. Porpoise, I wanted to say, because I thought that's how the tunamen spotted the fish. So I tried "the mammal that swims with the tuna." Either I said it wrong, or he didn't catch it, so I dropped the subject. Besides, even a schoolkid in Iowa knows "what about the porpoise." It started with the TV series *Flipper*, in which a smart, lovable dolphin played the role of a seagoing Lassie. And then came the movie, with actual footage of entire dolphin herds being trapped in the tunamen's nets unable to escape, innocent victims tangled and drowning in the nets or later hauled aboard the boat to a terrorized death on deck. The film told of an annual slaughter of three hundred thousand dolphins in the tuna fishery, and the outrage that swept the nation has rarely been equaled.

Stan Minisium, the man who was responsible for the film, is now living in the Bay Area working on the population dynamics of seals and sea lions, but the slaughter of the dolphins is still very much on his mind. Fifteen years ago, Stan was foundering in his third year of college when he read a short article on the tuna kill in *Time* magazine. Immediately he realized what he wanted to do. He quit school, marshalled a half dozen of his friends, and formed a nonprofit group called Save the Dolphin. In the process of gathering information on the subject, Stan came across a paper by the National Marine Fisheries Service biologist Bill Perrin. In the middle of the paper was a notation that there was film footage available of dolphins being captured and killed in the nets. That launched an idea that would take Save the Dolphin through as rough and unmanageable a tempest as ever is brewed on the sea, a journey that couldn't have begun with a more favorable and fortuitous wind.

Save the Dolphin set out to make a film around the footage Stan obtained from NMFS. At the same time, a reporter from the *Los Angeles Times* wrote an article about the many activities of the group, including a discussion of their plan. Stan's phone began ringing as soon as the paper hit the streets. Editors called from Hollywood to volunteer their services on the film, Dick Cavett volunteered to do the narration, Adolf Gasser's donated film equipment, Westinghouse Broadcasting Company supplied the camera crews, the Environmental Defense Fund raised $15,000, and in two years they had made the $70,000-film for $13,000. By 1979, the film had been shown by 250 TV stations over five hundred times to a viewing audience totaling over four hundred million people throughout the world. The film touched a moral nerve. So unquestionable was the evil, so unacceptable was the slaughter to so many Americans that in any part of the country you could count the bumper stickers, BOYCOTT TUNA, DON'T EAT FLIPPER.

The well of sentiment propelled Save the Dolphin to redouble its efforts, but the problem has never been solved. And as Stan looks back on the struggle, he is himself discouraged and puzzled. "NMFS knew about this kill all along, way before we got into it, but they were passive and apathetic. You have to understand that the people who work in an agency like this can get swallowed up in it; there's pressure if they talk, there's pressure just to do your job and present your papers. The director told me himself that if they started cracking down on the captains, they'd lose all cooperation from the industry for their observer program, or the boats would start registering under a foreign flag, which they're doing now anyway. And then the director of NMFS said to me that the industry will regulate their own problems, which, of course, they won't.

"It's no secret that 90 percent of the animals are killed by 15 percent of the captains. The industry itself calls them bad captains, but you'll never get a situation where one captain tells another captain what to do. There's ways to stop the kill when the set's good—the backdown procedure and the Medina panel* work pretty well if they take the time to do it right. Both these methods, by the way, were introduced by the fishermen. But most of the kills are during a bum set—say the current changes in the middle of a set and the net collapses.

"The only way to test new methods efficiently is to have your own vessel. But, you know, when the Marine Mammal Commission was first formed, what they did with the money was try to study the biology of the relationship of the dolphin and the tuna, and they still don't have an answer to that. There's been nobody out there to enforce the law, nobody out there at all. The observers were never given marshall status; they could look but not write. They could write down how many dolphin were released but not how many were killed. Then, later on, they could write how many were killed, but that information was later deleted from the reports as confidential.

"A lot of the observers hated the program anyway. They couldn't even wait to get back to the United States to get off the boats; they'd get off at Samoa or Costa Rica or anywhere, because

---

*A small-mesh web panel in the back of the net which prevents the dolphins from becoming entangled.

they were being ostracized on the boats. Now they're putting two observers on the boat and requiring that the captain meet with them every night, just to reduce this problem of being ostracized.

"Now they're saying the problem's solved because U.S. boats are killing only fifteen thousand to twenty-five thousand tuna a year. But that's because the herd is depleted. But you get five biologists that say the herd is depleted, and they'll get five that say it isn't.

"I got out because you can work in that capacity of rocking the boat for only so long, and one by one, all the doors that used to be open to you begin to close. I also got out because I'm completely perplexed. The problem isn't solved. I'm burned out."

Carlo walked me out to an upper deck where the speedboats are launched in the fast frenzy just prior to a set. The deck was about thirty feet above the water, with no rail or rope to keep you from walking right off the edge, which I nearly did. "Jesus," I said, "this is dangerous." I could imagine what it must be like with the boat pitching and yawing, the speedboats swinging on the end of the boom, and everybody yelling at everybody else to hurry up because the fish got tails, and no rail!

"Right," said Carlo, "we lost a guy over the side there once. It happens." He must have seen on my face that I was a little taken aback over his casual attitude and he said, "I thought you're a fisherman." It had been awhile, and I remembered how different it was at sea. He was right. The sun comes up and the sun goes down, and sometimes the ocean gives you fish and sometimes it takes a friend. It just happens.

Carlo started right in with another story about a guy who was lost on the last trip on one of the other boats. He was the guy they put in the water to check that there aren't any dolphins on the bottom of the net. Nobody saw the shark, which bit off part of his shoulder. The guy lived for three days, but it takes a lot longer than that to get back to port. *"Delfin,"* I said, "that's the word I was trying to think of before. What about the dolphins?"

"It works out pretty good if we have a decent set," said Carlo, "but if the net collapses we lose a lot of dolphins.

"This year hasn't been too bad, because we haven't been working with the dolphins. But for about the last ten years these dolphins have caused us nothing but trouble. Now we got to have these scientists come on the boats and it's bad. Everybody else on the boat is working like crazy to make a living, and this guy just stands there the whole trip doing nothing, just looking at you like you're the devil. But most of the guys figure that it's him that is the devil. A lot of the guys are very superstitious so nobody talks to him, and they string garlic and hang it around the door of his room to keep his spirit from getting onto the deck. But I don't believe in that; it doesn't make any difference what you do, those scientists are bad luck no matter what."

Carlo showed me around the engine room and through the refrigerated fish holds, and then we went back up past the chapel of the Virgin, where Carlo inconspicuously made the sign of the cross, and back into the galley, where he started to pour a couple more drinks. "No thanks," I said. "I have to get back."

"I'll drive you," he insisted. "Too many sharks out there," and he laughed.

We weren't three minutes into the late-night throb of North Harbor Drive when a shiny black car pulled in front of us. "Hey, look at that," I said, pointing to his bumper sticker that read NUKE THE WHALES. I translated as best I could, "It says to throw a nuclear bomb on the whales." Carlo looked at me from a million miles away in his limbo between satellites and superstition. He was completely perplexed, "Why would anyone want to say that?"

And, having been instantly replanted into the cynicism of the streets, I was thinking, "Man, if you've been in California for twenty-seven years, and you don't understand media hype, then there's no way I could explain it even if you spoke perfect English."

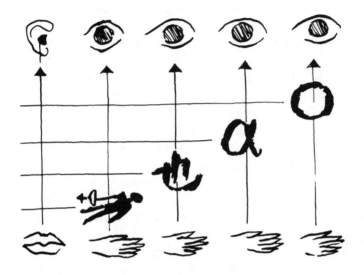

Chapter 38

Dolphin Talk

Since I quit fishing I've been working with kids: abused, abandoned, and neglected kids, as they're called on the county dockets.
(I've been doing this because I've found that writing is more an
expense than an income.) When the kids first come to us in resi-
dential treatment, many of them have what we call an "uncle in
Texas"—someone far away and out of reach. But, says the kid,
this person understands him, speaks his language; this is the person who is going to rescue him. And though the person really
exists, the rest is a fantasy. Although the relationship fills a need,
the very worst thing you can do is encourage it, because as long as
the kid believes in it, he's never going to form real relationships

with the people around him, real relationships that have hardships and misunderstandings but ultimately the chance for love.

Every one of us in this society is severely deprived of a relationship with Mother Nature. Nature no longer provides for us, no longer supplies the rhythm of our lives; nor is it the source of our work or any interaction at all other than the camping, hiking, and sailing which is only the hollow shell of the real relationship we lost generations ago. The loss and the need are as great as life itself, because our minds, bodies, and souls were designed as a template to nature. And our lives no longer fit.

So we create a fantasy. We look out to the sea, which is still primal and unknown, and we say the dolphin is going to talk to us; the dolphin has an ideal society; the dolphin is playful and nurturing; the dolphin is love.

A friend of mine said he had a religious experience after seeing a whale. He's the same friend who won't go fishing with me because he doesn't want to kill anything. I say to him, "Richard, you've got some serious denial going on about what nature is all about."

One time we went to the beach, and a sea lion was propped against a rock, dying, and Richard said, "We've got to get it to a rehabilitation center right now!"

"But," I said, "that animal is supposed to die to keep the species strong."

And he became very upset with me and said, "You've killed so many animals that you're starting to think that death is natural."

I know that the leaders of the environmental movement understand that it's not the dolphin, or the seal, or the otter that have to be saved; it's the roundness of things, it's nature in its full spectrum of dynamics. I know this because I've talked with many leaders of various groups. So I ask them, "Why? Why this sentimental thing with the marine mammals?" And the answer is always the same, "To pull the people in." But I think it is dangerous because it only promotes the fantasy.

It's true that this tremendous love of marine mammals expresses people's real and deep desire for a relationship and renewal with nature. But it's a dysfunctional projection in terms of survival, and it needs to be disillusioned so that real change can come about. As long as people are focused in this fantasy, they're not going to deal with the fact that it's their own way of life that deprives them of interaction with nature, and talking with the dolphin will not magically re-establish the link. Because the dolphin is not the deity, and the fisherman is not the devil.

The fisherman is out there every day, working and dealing with these animals. He sees that the dolphin has teeth and spends much of its day corralling schools of fish, trapping them up against the surface, and then decimating the school. And the fisherman sees that the dolphin is curious and comes up to his boat, and he talks to the dolphin, in the same way he talks to the salmon and the sun and the wind and the sea gulls and the slime eels. But this communication is not romanticized; sometimes the fisherman is enraged with the interaction, and at times he is thrilled with its bounty, and humiliated and terrified and cocky and disgusted and in awe—in other words, the full range of human interaction in mesh with the full range of nature's expression.

So when the fisherman sees the public coming out on the ocean to adore the mammals, he sees it as a cult, as "Bambiology," as totally out of touch with reality, the same way you would see vanloads of people coming into your neighborhood to adore the dog. And the fisherman recoils at joining forces with this fantasy, because there is so much more going on.

The fisherman knows intuitively that his way of life—despite the nets, the hook, and the harpoon—is much closer to a way of life that is necessary for the preservation of the earth than that of the person who lives every day with artificial things created by destroying the earth—and then on weekends goes to sea to worship the whale.

Chapter 39

To Hunt or to Farm

It has long been a collective belief of human beings that we didn't become civilized until we replaced hunting and gathering with agriculture. Recently, as we began looking to the sea for many of our needs, we noticed the fishermen out there, still chasing after wild fish just like the nomads of old, and it was embarrassing, a gross anachronism in a modern world. Simultaneously, aquaculture was heralded as the dazzling hope in a bleak world of depleted fisheries and failing agricultures. And during the 1970s, throughout the world, its development was funded accordingly.

The last dozen years have unfolded a fascinating story of modern man's attempt to catch up two thousand years in the cul-

turing of fish. Not surprisingly, many of its dramatic moments
have taken place in California. But first, we take a brief jaunt to
Southeast Asia, for it was there, in the underdeveloped coast-
lands, that our dream was inflated with hope. Southeast Asians
have been raising fish as an integral part of their survival for over
two thousand years.

In Vietnam, Taiwan, Thailand, Malaysia, Indonesia, southern
China, Singapore, the Philippines, among the great populations
of people we hardly know, fish is the main source of animal protein, and 25 percent of this fish is produced on the farm. Says Tom
Hendrick, a California aquaculture specialist who recently returned from Taiwan, "You stand by their ponds and look in any
direction as far as the eye can see, and you see more and more
ponds; and you drive for miles and miles, and you see more
ponds. It sure puts into perspective what we call aquaculture
here." A closer look at these ponds will also provide the background for an understanding of what went wrong with the dream.

One of the more interesting and traditional methods of Asian
fish culture takes place right in the rice fields and doubles the yield
of the land. Rice plants are usually grown in four to five inches of
standing water. Fish often inhabit the paddies quite naturally;
their larvae or eggs flow in with the water when the irrigation
ditches are opened to the fields. The base of the rice plants form an
ideal matrix for the spontaneous growth of algae, worms, insects,
and small crustaceans, a veritable smorgasbord of gourmet fish
foods. It was an obvious step for the farmers to simply add more
larvae of carp or mullet or any one of a dozen other fish that do
well in the paddies and greatly increase their yield. When the
ponds are drained to harvest the rice, there also is a harvest of fat-
tened fish, the complete and nutritious diet of millions of Asian
peoples.

The mullet and milkfish of Southeast Asia are worth some
special attention as they are being held up as the kind of fish that
would be ideal for culture around the world. They're fast-growing;
they can tolerate broad swings of salinity and temperature; and
most attractive of all, they eat right off the bottom of the food
chain. All you have to do is give them a shallow pond and let the
sun shine in. Algae blooms in the sun; the fish eat the algae; and

presto, you have protein in one easy step. Naturally the fish farmers have refined their techniques over the hundreds of years to ensure optimum quality of the algal mat and ideal conditions for the fish. But the fact remains: with the most primitive tools and almost no overhead, these farmers can average a production of four hundred pounds of fish per acre per year. When it comes to protein, our most sophisticated agricultural technology can hardly compete.

The Southeast Asians have become adept at raising a great variety of fishes, eels, shrimps, and other crustaceans. It would be impossible here to give even a cursory overview of their techniques. But one more fish will help explain the status of aquaculture today.

The tilapia, a native of Africa, was introduced by an old Chinese fish fancier into his exotic aquarium collection. About sixty years ago a couple of the fish got out and began multiplying throughout the streams of Asia, spreading from one country to the next. It wasn't long before this prolific little animal was pegged for culture. Today no fish is more commonly cultured in the world, with the possible exception of carp. The tilapia grows anywhere and eats anything, which may sound a might exaggerated. But all you have to do is watch them, happy as clams, swimming and growing in a stagnant ditch of water among piles of garbage, and you'll probably be inspired to the same conclusion as many culturists—"This is the fish that's going to save the world!" In addition to its hardiness, the tilapia's meat has the requisite high-quality protein; it also has the highest fat content of any culturable fish, a fact that won't impress the American market, but in third world countries, this is the fat of life. Some culturists are so entranced with the tilapia that they believe this must be the fish used by Jesus in the miracle of the multiplication of the fishes.

So why is two thirds of the world starving?

One: The fish farming that has been practiced by the Southeast Asians for two thousand years is not true aquaculture, not in the sense of agriculture where you raise a chicken, the chicken lays an egg, you eat the chicken, but there's still the egg to hatch into another chicken. The Asian fish farmers are dependent on collecting wild larvae to stock their ponds. They don't have control of the fish's total life cycle, and in most cases, the baseline knowledge doesn't even exist. It took a mountain of money and ten years of intensive research just to get an old run-of-the-mill mullet to breed in captivity. And that's still miles from production scale. Fish are very different from the air-breathing animals we've domesticated for thousands of years. The conditions required for their breeding, their complex life cycles, their many larval stages with changing nutritional needs, are completely foreign to those of us who are used to baby pigs that look like, act like, and eat like mama pig.

Two: The Asian estuaries and tidelands where the larvae stocks have traditionally been collected are being industrialized and polluted. The adult wild fish are overfished. Since World War II, there has been a growing and very serious crisis in Southeast Asian aquaculture, because the larvae are increasingly difficult to obtain.

Three: Western countries have insisted on helping the people of Southeast Asia beef up their production of rice with pesticides and machinery. Every pesticide we have introduced kills the fish in the ponds; heavy machinery requires that the ponds be drained so often that the fish don't have time to reach maturity. The practice of raising fish in rice ponds is steadily on the decline.

Four: Aquaculture is an art, much more so than agriculture. Some individuals are very successful at it, but you cannot just watch the farmer for a while, take notes, dig your own pond, and repeat his techniques. That farmer is attuned to so many things about the subtleties of his local weather, the feel of his water, the texture of his soil, the behavior of his fish, the smell of the air, there's no way you can repeat what he's doing unless you spend the better part of a lifetime following in his footsteps—just the way he followed his father when he was a kid. But nowadays these kids are sent off to school so they'll be educated, and the immeasurably valuable local knowledge that has been gathered through centuries is lost in one generation—forever. The kid takes a course on modern aquaculture techniques that explores the operations of million-dollar farms; he goes back to the land; and lo and behold, he doesn't make it. We send over more advisors and technicians to help them some more, and lo and behold, more people are starving than ever. All because we know very little about their animals, even less about labor-intensive techniques, and absolutely nothing about subsistence.

Five: "Technological research has never been interested in feeding the starving masses." So said the director of an acquacultural institute who, not surprisingly, didn't want me to use his name. Nothing could be more obvious. Of all the millions of dollars funneled into aquaculture in the last decade, the vast majority of it has been targeted on the culture of luxury items like Malaysian prawns, lobsters, salmon, and abalone. The same companies that went into these countries and destroyed their agricultural self-sufficiency with the monolithic cropping of pineapple, sugar cane, and coffee have now invaded their aquaculture with capital-intensive industries producing a crop that the local people can't afford to eat. And to top it off, these programs have even failed to produce profits, because aquaculture is still an art.

What about tilapia, the miracle fish? Well, they're working on it in many parts of the world. But many of tilapia's most charming attributes have been added to aquaculture's list of dilemmas. Tilapia reproduces on a wet dime, and it keeps on reproducing, and unless you can keep them from reproducing, they use up all their energy making more tilapia instead of growing. Tilapia's heralded hardiness has been the plague of almost every country where it has been introduced. It has destroyed the streams and estuaries because the native fish cannot compete. The tilapia also invades the mullet and milkfish ponds and destroys the algal mat. Tilapia was brought into Hawaii by the Department of Fish and Game to control the mosquito; mention tilapia now, and watch the look that crosses a Hawaiian's face. And in California, if you want the Fish and Game to forget about asking to see your expired fishing license, just mumble a little something about your pet tilapia.

Which brings us neatly back to California, where, naturally, our surge of interest in aquaculture has encountered the paradoxes inherent in the Asian methods. Indeed, the problems generated by pesticides, urbanized estuaries, and tidelands; the disease that comes from attempts to intensify culture; the competition for water use—these are all amplified as we try to fit the culture of wild fish into our way of life. In addition, we have no experience with wild animals. The pigs, chickens, cows, and goats we work with on the farm are only one part true animal. The other part is manufactured, a product of hundreds of years of genetic engineering, which has designed and redesigned the creature so that when we say jump, it jumps. It's been many generations since we have had to exercise that part of our own being that can mesh with and nurture growth on the wild side. It's been generations since practicing the art of nature has meant anything more than admiring its beauty.

No doubt California (and a few other states climatically suited for the culture of fish, like Hawaii, Louisiana, Mississippi) will continue to press forward toward the solutions to aquaculture's many problems. And not unpredictably, these efforts are targeted on altering the animals' genetics, finding new chemicals to control diseases, nutritional pumping (overfeeding), getting control of life cycles, and mechanization on the farms. And it's going to be a long road. The few successes you may have read about are generally propped up by large government or industrial funds. There are a few exceptions, of course, and they will be the subject of the next chapters. But for the most part, aquaculture in California today is more a tone of voice than a viable means of production.

Here are a few of the comments I heard upon bringing up the subject to a variety of experts:

A marine economist: "Oh, yes, aquaculture, the perennial gold at the end of the rainbow."

A researcher (when asked about a glowing report he had written on aquaculture's progress): "That's how you keep the grants rolling in. Uh, that's off the record, of course."

An ocean fisheries scientist: "The biggest question of all is, How do you make aquaculture pay its own way? Yes, I know, it's been a great media event."

Another fisheries scientist: "It [aquaculture] is the coming thing. That's what I told my kids when we first got into this, and now, that's what I'm telling my grandkids." And he laughed.

Chapter 40
Catfish Farm

Anyone who can make a go of aquaculture as a business has to be credited with having accomplished a formidable task. But how do you account for someone like George Ray, his brother, Leo, and his sister, Fern? With no previous experience, they bought some land in 1968 and dug out the ponds, and today they are producing over a half million pounds of catfish a year—30 percent of the total catfish production in the state of California. In addition, their farm is uniquely self-sufficient, from the spawning, rearing, and production right through to the marketing, trucking, and sales.

Now, catfish, to be sure, is a freshwater fish and as such is a little outside the range of this book. But at present, all marine fish production in California is still in the experimental stage and will likely remain there until the risks are reduced. Not that freshwater farming is a blue chip stock, by no means. And what it takes for George and his family to brew success in the freshwater ponds are exactly the same ingredients that will be required with fish of the sea.

"My brother and I were teaching high school up in the L.A. area. I was teaching math and science, and Leo was teaching science and photography. He wanted a change, I guess is the best way to put it. He'd worked at a fish research station while he was in college, and he started to think about growing fish. His initial thought was to work with tilapia because that's the fish they were working with at the research station. But in the course of investigating, we found that the catfish industry had begun to get off the ground in Arkansas and Mississippi, so we felt they afforded the best opportunity. Our sister Fern initially supplied some of the capital, and then she joined the operation full-time about five years ago. We decided on the Imperial Valley; we purchased some land in December 1968, began pond production in 1969, and had our first crop of fish that same year.

"Catfish culture began about twenty-five years ago in the southeastern states because the commercial fishermen had over-fished the natural stock. That's why the industry got its start back in Arkansas and Mississippi; the markets already existed, and the bankers were willing to take the risks. In fact our number one problem getting started here in California was the difficulty of getting capital; a lot of bankers out here had never even heard of aquaculture. We ended up having to depend on our own financing and borrowing from our family.

"The catfish has turned out to be a good choice for a lot of reasons. In the wild, they live in the fast-running water of small streams, and nobody thought they would tolerate a pond, but they're doing very well. It turns out they withstand a broad range of oxygen, temperature, and even salinity levels. They're hardy. We have to aerate the ponds, but we don't have to circulate the water. The first year we had a catastrophic loss due to a parasite infection that went through the fish when the water temperature dropped below sixty degrees. Maybe we could have prevented it if we'd had more experience, but it's hard to say, it happened so suddenly. We've been real lucky since then, until this year when we've been losing some fish to a buildup of ammonia in the ponds. The ammonia is always there as a metabolite of the fish, but I think the problem now is we're not getting enough wind to blow it off.

"Another good thing about the catfish is that its reproduction is easy to control, unlike the tilapia. In the wild, the male selects a protected area—a hole, a log, or roots in a tree—a cavelike affair into which he seduces the female. She lays her eggs, and then he kicks her out. Ten days later the eggs hatch, and for the next five days, the male swims with and protects his young brood; then his maternal instinct disappears. What's useful to us about all this is that if you have a smooth-bottomed pond, the animals won't spawn, and we can keep all their energy channeled into growth. And when we do want a spawn we transfer them to a special pond that we fill with ten-gallon cream cans which the males make into caves.

"The thing I like about this business is the lack of routine; every day is different, and every day is something new. I like the fact that there's a lot of unsolved problems, not just with the fish but with the laws and the regulations. The marketing end has been very interesting too. At first we sold mostly to recreational lakes, but slowly we developed our food market in the Asian communities. They like their fish fresh, and they like it even better live. Now over 90 percent of our fish goes to the food market. I really like the fish too. The catfish is a very intelligent animal, and it's easy to get attached to them. They learn quickly; you can teach them to eat out of a self-feeder in a matter of minutes. They also have a highly developed sensory system; they're very sensitive to smell and very sensitive to electric fields; they're very sensitive to the environment that they're in.

"To a large degree it's a seat-of-the-pants operation. How much you feed a fish is an art rather than a science. We don't measure out so many pellets a day for the fish. The people doing the feeding have the authority and the responsibility for deciding how much they put out based on their observations of the response they get when they begin the feeding operation. And if one pond is not feeding well, then it's their responsibility to find out why, to spend some extra time watching those fish, and sample a couple, and look in the microscope—whatever it takes. I have a crew of seven people, and I'm partial to people who have been in the Peace Corps because they already know what it is to be on their own.

"It's hard to pinpoint any one thing that has made our farm a success. Our success in marketing has a lot to do with it. Not that we devoted a lot of time and money to marketing, that's not it. It's the fact that we sought out and found out some good market niches. And then there's the hard work and the fact that we're up at dawn every morning checking every pond. But the biggest thing, I think, is the fact that we live right here on the farm. The fish come first, and we plan our lives around them rather than the other way around—rather than incorporating the fish into our lives—seven days a week, twenty-four hours a day."

Chapter 41

Striped Bass in the Power Plant

If George Ray has shown with his catfish farm that aquaculture in California can wedge out a piece of the pie, Aquatic Systems Incorporated in San Diego has shown that aquaculture can also have a very sharp cutting edge. ASI started twenty years ago as a small research firm, and since then they have worked on the culture of over ninety different species of fish. They have contracted with the Nigerian government on the development of tilapia farms, with the California Department of Fish and Game on abalone culture, with the International Investment and Trust Bank on development of aquaculture systems for the Caribbean, with Sea Grant on the development of ocean ranching of coho salmon, with the Jet Propulsion Labs on growing freshwater shrimp in geothermal water. And these are only five out of over fifty pioneering projects around the world that have brought the leaders of ASI as close as anyone to a realistic view of the shape of aquaculture's future in California. This is what they see, as condensed from a discussion with Jim Carlberg, ASI's vice president.

The major factors are (1) aquaculture in California cannot be labor-intensive but can be capital-intensive, so will certainly be directed at markets of high profitability; (2) California's climatic capacity to raise tropical species or to match tropical production is considered only marginal—and then only in southern California; (3) land, water, and laws are tighter in California than anywhere else in the world, and the same is true of environmental constraints. Given this picture, animals like lobster, abalone, shrimp, and striped bass appear prominent, as do cement ponds and raceways, high-density culture, high technology—and all of it finding its home in some very unexpected niches. Like the striped bass in the power plant project. Though it sounds more like an image you might have in the semicomatose throes of a fever, this is actually a widely accepted concept throughout the coastal United States, a concept pioneered to a large extent by ASI and backed by the power plants themselves.

Coastal power plants use seawater as coolant; they use in the neighborhood of a million gallons a minute. When the water is pumped back into the ocean, at that same rate of a million gallons a minute, it is 20 degrees Fahrenheit hotter than the ambient temperature. This kind of temperature change is scalding in a marine environment, where even a one- or two-degree change can throw the whole thing out of balance, and the stigma of thermal polluter was added to the power plants' many other stigmas. But the power companies, being masters of stigma inversion, had a few meetings and said, Ok, boys, what we have to do with this situation is put this hot water to use, and then we have here what will henceforth be called a thermal resource. The Southern California Gas and Electric striped bass project is only one of many such projects taking place in California power plants.

In 1973, Sea Grant supplied the major funding, ASI provided the developmental capability, and SCG & E put up the land and the "tropical current." After lengthy consideration, the striped bass was chosen as the animal most likely to succeed. Its marketability is proven. The fish is hardy and tolerates all salinities from fresh to full-strength seawater (except for the first six weeks of life, when it requires fresh water). The hatchery biology for the striped bass is known, which is unique among marine fin fishes in California, most of whose life cycles have not been fully determined. But the striped bass, like the salmon, is anadromous—it spawns in fresh water—and as such its reproductive cycle is more susceptible to study and control. The striped bass is also a schooling fish that inhabits the full water column, which means it will fully utilize the deep tanks of intensive culture systems.

The decision to do intensive culture was automatic, given the cost of land in California. Pond rearing would require three hundred to four hundred acres for even a small operation, and if you ever got your hands on that much land in southern California you'd build condominiums, not ponds. Not only that, but the large surface area of traditional pond systems would lose too much heat at night. Solving the problems that derive from intensive culturing is not so automatic; in fact, the problems that develop when you crowd one pound of fish into a gallon of water constitute major constraints to the growth of aquaculture in California.

In a pond, the natural soil bacteria remove the waste metabolites of the fish. In intensive culture, these metabolites quickly build up to poisonous levels, and fail-safe filtration systems have to be developed. In intensive culture you can't depend on natural oxygenation. The natural pond is a much more resilient system in many ways. The tanks are subject to sudden and catastrophic losses, not only in the event of systems failures, but also because crowding causes tremendous stress for a fish and leads to disease. Many of these diseases have never been seen before, and most of them are transmitted in a way described by all aquaculturists as explosive. Crowding also increases the cannibalistic tendencies in the fish, necessitating meticulous size classing in the tanks. The key to forestalling most of the other problems is maintaining excellent water quality, eternal vigilance, constant temperature, and an undiluted flow of good luck. The technology was developed;

the water was pumped into six eight-foot-diameter tanks each six feet deep; and they were ready for the fish.

Forty million one- to two-inch striped bass fingerlings are raised every year at the Fish and Game's Elkhorn hatchery, mostly for mitigation, but some are sold to aquaculture. (The fingerlings are raised in ponds because so far intensive culture has been unsuccessful. For some as yet unknown reason, young raised in the tanks will not develop normal swim bladders, and as a result, the fish expend all their energy swimming up because they can't control their buoyancy.) So in 1982, over six thousand pond-reared fingerlings were trucked into San Diego where they first had to be slowly acclimated to the full-strength seawater and high temperatures they were about to inhabit at the Encina power plant.

Now right along here there ought to be a nagging question in your mind. Why go to all this trouble to get hot water? Earlier in this book didn't we extol the fertility of cold, upwelled waters? Good question. Upwelled water is loaded with nitrates and phosphates, the two essential nutrients whose shortage limits populations over so much of the ocean. Cold water also holds more oxygen than warm water and can sustain larger blooms of plankton. But if you artificially pump hot water with oxygen and the necessary nutrients, fish will grow much faster than in the cold water. This is because the fish is a cold-blooded animal. In the wilds of the Chesapeake Bay and the central and south Atlantic where the striped bass is native, it takes three years for the fish to reach a one-pound weight. The plan and hope at the power plant was to bring the fish to the one-pound weight in less than a year, thereby inducing the most interesting phenomenon of all—good cash flow. The 1982 experiment was a resounding success. ASI produced six thousand one-pound striped bass in less than a year, proving the viability of their methods beyond a doubt.

Commercialization was the next step, requiring the installation of twenty-six more tanks to bring production levels up to four hundred thousand pounds a year. Commercialization also requires financial backing, but ASI is not willing to take the risk. They're going to continue raising striped bass for sale, but they're going to do it in the freshwater thermal ponds in the Coachella Valley. This way, if something goes wrong they can immediately cover themselves by putting catfish in the freshwater ponds. Nothing actually went wrong at the Encina power plant; it's just at this stage in the game the success of intensive fish culture in saltwater depends too much on good luck. And in part, the good luck they had at Encina was due to the fact that they didn't have any bad luck.

But as Jim Carlberg points out, the day is coming. In addition he notes, "At this point we can't compete with the fishermen, but with the fishermen's increasing costs, regulations, and depletions, aquaculture will automatically come into its economic own." Aquaculture, like agriculture, also has the advantage of controlling the size and date of delivery.

"Won't it end up being like the tasteless tomato?" I asked.

"This is one disadvantage of aquaculture right now," says Jim. "A cultured fish will never taste like a wild fish, because a wild fish eats so many different foods. But we're learning ways to tailor the texture and taste of the aquaculture fish. Genetic manipulation will be important, too."

As for the power plants, the potential of the tropical current is not forgotten. In fact, Southern California Edison right now has lobster growing at its Oxnard plant. And other utilities along the coast are expressing interest. Only one little problem—even at maximum production such as that projected by ASI, aquaculture will only be using about 3,000 gallons a minute of hot water. That means 3,000 gallons of thermal resource and 997,000 gallons yet of thermal pollution.

Chapter 42

Roll Over, Hippocrates

He ignores the first ring of the telephone; second ring, and his conscience nags; third ring, and professionalism prevails. It doesn't take John Modin long to gather up his bag and hop into the small plane that ferries him to the remotest parts of the state. By the hundredth time, he could do it in his sleep.

This time he's headed to the backwoods country of the Mad River in northern California. Because of the population density up there, this is the last place he wanted to see an outbreak of disease. But when John arrived, he took one look at the exophthalmos (bulging eyes), the bloated bellies, and the listless behavior, and immediately his mind told him he was looking at an epidemic of

IHN, a viral disease he'd seen many times before. But like all good diagnosticians, John also listened to his gut, and he had a feeling that something here just didn't fit. Before jumping to any conclusions he wanted to check it out back at the lab. He took the necessary samples, and sure enough, they were negative for IHN. That's when he noticed something weird in the kidneys, something he had never seen before. But there wasn't much time to figure it out. John had two million patients all coming down with the same thing.

Roll over, Hippocrates, there's a whole new school of fish doctors on the scene, and the reason is that there's a lot more sick fish, and these sick fish are another serious problem for aquaculture. When fish are crowded they get sick. Not only that, but too often the farmer comes to realize there's something wrong only when he walks out to the pond in the morning and gets hit between the eyes with the sight of every last fish floating belly up to the sky. "Just because they live in a damned school," says the broken farmer to no one in particular, "don't sit with me they gotta die in a damned school." And then he calls the fish doctor, and they stand at the edge of the pond shaking their heads together. Because most of the time, the diseases that kill these fish are brand new to the books.

Actually, it's only been since the late 1970s that doctoral programs have been offered in fish pathology, though the profession is a few decades older than that. Bob Bush got his bachelor's degree in zoology and his master's in public health microbiology. And for a while he studied bubonic plague in wildlife. "What country were you working in?" I asked, hoping for an exotic tale of steamy swamps in some tropic hellhole on the other side of the earth.

"What country?" he repeated, a little puzzled. "I was in the United States. You know, there's so much of it around in the wild that if we ever had a natural disaster that broke down our standard of living, we'd have a major outbreak on our hands."

Bob went back to school to get his Ph.D. in immunology, and he did his thesis on developing serological tests for diagnosing diseases in wild fish. After that came a job at Humboldt State as assistant professor of fish and wildlife pathology. From there Bob wanted to try his hand in private practice. He now specializes

in trout on commercial farms, developing vaccines for fish, re-
searching their diseases, and working with their genetics. "I love
this field," says Bob. "It's one of the most fascinating jobs there is.
Every day I go to work, I see things that nobody has ever seen
before, and I do things that nobody has ever done before. A lot of
people in this field feel the same way. It's very alive, very active
work. Fish medicine is developing in some very different ways
from other animal medicine. For example, live vaccines aren't
very useful because we don't dare put them in the water. More
and more we are having to go to a genetic approach to disease
resistance."

In addition to the problems of starting from scratch just in the
description of diseases for this very young science, fish medicine is
at the same time having to deal with many of the problems common to all twentieth-century medicine. Bob recently chaired a
week-long conference with the Food and Drug Administration
about the problem of drug laws and regulations, a problem that,
ironically, hits fish pathologists more than anyone. "It costs eight
million dollars and takes six years of research before the FDA will
accept a drug to be put into the field. This is true even if the drug
has already been approved for another animal. The drug companies bear the brunt of this cost, which, of course, they hope to
make back in sales—which in the case of a drug to be used on fish
just doesn't compute."

Another issue probably would never cross your mind unless
you were a veterinarian or a fish contemplating a malpractice suit
—that is the question of practicing medicine without a license.
Some of the people in this field are vets, but the majority of fish
doctors come from a microbiology, immunology, or virology
background. "Back East," says Bob, "this business of practicing
without a license has been more of a problem, but out here in the
West there has been a very healthy cooperation among all groups
involved. People are working together, and it's important that we
continue to do so, as disease is a major constraint to the development and profitability of aquaculture."

And as everyone I talked to confirmed, the number one cause
of disease outbreaks in fish is crowding. "We're finding that a lot
of these diseases are carried in the wild population, but they re-

main asymptomatic until you crowd them. Crowding is a very stressful situation for a fish. Another stress that is put on the fish in the aquacultural situation is that they are pushed nutritionally to grow fast. Because of these problems, many people are beginning to rethink the strategy of using hatcheries to replenish wild stocks. There's no question that it would be better to destroy the hatcheries in favor of restoring the environment, but in many cases that's just not possible. And, of course, in aquaculture, where you need to make a profit, we just have to find our way through these diseases."

As attempts are being made to bring more and more marine animals into high-production culture, more and more diseases are being generated in the ponds, including unusual diseases of lobsters, shrimps, and prawns. Recent intensive efforts to culture striped bass are still being held back in the early stage by an as yet undiagnosed phenomenon that causes sudden death to the entire school. So far, this disease is simply being referred to as the "larval crash."

The state Department of Fish and Game has put together a fish pathology lab in Sacramento to try to control these new diseases. They have a staff of five pathologists, and they are inundated. Their job is to keep tabs on all outbreaks of disease in the state, to check that any fish coming into the state is disease free, and to ensure that when disease does break out, measures are taken to keep domestic fish from infecting wild stocks. Sometimes this means destroying all the fish in the pond.

That was the decision finally made by John Modin with his two million fish on the Mad River. "We got stumped by that disease for a long time," says John, "until we found in a search of the literature that this disease had been seen before in Idaho and in Europe. It's called proliferative kidney disease. It had never been seen before in California. And we never wanted to see it again. It had already killed the majority of the two million fish, and we decided to destroy the rest to avoid the possibility of having the disease spread (except for a handful of survivors, which we wanted to bring back here to the lab for further study.)"

"What did you find out about those survivors?" I asked him in a later phone call.

"Are you kidding?" said John. "We're busy. I just had to destroy another whole batch of fish in Calaveras County that came down with whirling disease. It's a parasite that affects the cartilage, and because the semicircular canal is partly cartilaginous, the fish lose their sense of direction and swim in a whirling fashion. There's no cure for this one, and there probably never will be. As for studying those fish from the Mad River," he said, leaving no doubt how kindred this profession is to the practice of medicine everywhere, "I don't have time to breathe."

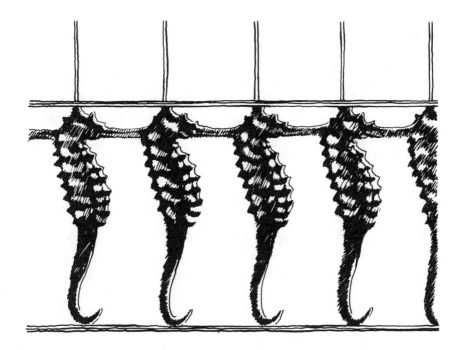

Chapter 43

Steinhart Aquarium

Given the headaches of raising just one species of fish in an artificial environment, can you imagine the daily crises in the care and feeding of fourteen hundred different species of fish that hail from all over the world? Fourteen thousand fish in over five hundred tanks and only twenty-six workers to share the burden. And can you imagine how severe must be the disposition of the one in charge, a dogged old gentlemen, bent over from having abandoned all the fun of life just to oversee the solution of every new crisis? But wrong! Meet John McCosker, director of Steinhart Aquarium since 1974.

"I was a southern California beach boy. I grew up in L.A.

having to work to get to the beach and go nuts looking into the tide pools, picking up the crabs and getting bit on the finger. Then I got into snorkeling; then I found out about wet suits. That was really the living end when I found out you could be warm, too. And then I found out about Mexico and tropical waters!

"I grew up as a kid doing all this stuff. I was lucky. I had some good advice and smart parents who convinced me to get a really good solid education. And at college, a couple of key people along the way said, 'Hey, live to work, don't work to live,' which I've done ever since.

"I went to Scripps Institute for graduate school and lived like a rat, eating lobster and abalone because I couldn't afford ground round. I fished all the time I was a student, working at night and fishing during the day when I didn't have class. After a couple of years, I got tired of being a student and got a fellowship to go to Panama and work with the shrimp fishermen doing a survey prior to the planned construction of the sea-level canal.

"Then I went to Peru and Ecuador to work on some projects there, had a good time, came back, finished my degree, and went to Australia. One morning in Sydney, I was reading the paper with breakfast, and there was a paragraph saying that the man who ran Steinhart had died. I thought, 'Oh what a shame,' and never thought about it again because I didn't know the man. I finished up my work there, went back to the States and got a phone call. 'You want to run an aquarium?' I said, 'What's an aquarium?' They were willing to risk the chance of my making a real mess here. They wanted a young scientist who hadn't been raised with the biases that the aquarium had. They figured you can teach the aquarium business to a scientist, but you can't teach science to an aquarist.

"I was twenty-seven when I got the job. I was the youngest guy on the staff. Twenty-six guys older than me. I was very nervous about it, and so were they. The first thing I did was to hire some young guys.

"I didn't have a green thumb, either, but that's not my job. I sit here in this office and think up ridiculous questions like 'Hasn't anyone thought of putting penguins in hot water? What about an exhibit of fish-eating bass?'

"What great fun for me to do it! What great luck! I've committed my entire life to it. I go home every night and read and write till I can't keep my eyes open. Then four or five hours later I get up and start again.

"Steinhart Aquarium is the grand dame of American aquariums. It was built in 1923. The concept was a great underwater zoo, a gorgeous experience in the French tradition, where you walk underground in a grotto with exotic creatures from the Amazon, from Tahiti, and incredibly bizarre places that people only read about in books. That's what they set out to do, and in the process they did some very clever things that were never done before—transported sharks on ships, brought golden trout out of the high Sierra by mule—pioneering stuff. They also spawned a generation of kids who wanted to be, not oceanographers, because that term didn't even exist then, but fishkeepers. Before Jacques Costeau was on TV, how else did you find out about this incredible world? This aquarium helped make people ready for oceanography; it was a step in the evolution of our consciousness of things underwater.

"Today we have a million and a half people coming through here every year. And you look every night before you close the doors, and there are so many handprints and noseprints on the glass of the tanks—for that reason we made a conscious decision not to have shows, not to have dancing porpoises and fiery hoops and animals jumping through them. The animals themselves are so exciting, why degrade them?

"We have over fourteen thousand fish here. How do you take care of them? First, you hire smart people that know how to do it. Some people have a sixth sense, a blue thumb. Some people around here are just geniuses about fish, psychic about fish, Dr. Doolittles—they talk to the fish. I've assembled a team that's here because they love it. How do I find them? They come to us; they hang around; they have no experience other than being lifelong naturalists. There's no one on the staff with my kind of education. You don't learn how to keep fish alive in school—it's a seat-of-the-pants operation. You just have that magic touch with animals or you don't.

"A lot of these animals that come here, nobody knows anything about. We learn by trial and error with each fish. How do you know what to feed them? Well, you open their mouths and see what kind of teeth they have; you see how long their stomach is; you use horse sense. No doubt it's complex. We have over nine major water systems, each with a different salinity, temperature, pH, and so on, and then we have another dozen subsystems.

"Any problems? Like the winter disaster of 1983, during the great highway sewer construction, when they accidentally (because nobody talked to each other), they accidentally dumped the tailings onto our beach collector. But we didn't know. We just started seeing animals die. We did tests for everything—phenols, salinity, oxygen, temperature—but it was just too subtle at first. Then the fish started dying like crazy. Then we discovered that aquifer fresh water was leaking in, and we were getting clobbered. Then we had to convince the city that they had too much invested in this aquarium to just let it die. That was our biggest problem, the political end.

"Fortunately, Mayor Feinstein is a smart lady who said that if the city aquarium were to go down, that would be terrible for a city depending on tourism and education. We got the money together, talked to all the agencies involved, and they were saying, 'Well, you better file form 22AB.' And I said, 'Well, the fish are dying, goddammit; forget these forms,' and finally somebody had some sense and said, 'Well, OK, we have this emergency measure here . . .' and we solved it!

"Now we have a very reliable system here, and we're in great shape till the next big mistake. But in the process we lost dozens and dozens of animals. And there was one real tragedy, very sad. We lost our old grouper, old Ulysses, he'd been here since the early fifties. Poor old Ulysses cacked because of a kidney failure, because of the stress of the water change.

"My main striving for this aquarium is to bring things in that people would never ever see, animals beyond the bread and butter of this business, things like flashlight fish, deep sea fish, and so on. We've had the only living white shark ever held in captivity. It was a frisky young shark that was in good shape because Al Wilson, who caught it, was a very savvy fisherman and took care of it. She wasn't only doing well; she was getting better in the tank.

Then we discovered this incredible thing about white sharks and how sensitive they are to electric fields. She started banging her head against this one spot in the tank where there was an electric leak. We didn't know it at the time, but there was a point one two five millivolt difference, and it excited her enough so she thought she was feeding on something. She was attacking the electric field discharge, which is the same thing a struggling prey gives off, and in the process she was injuring herself badly.

"It was four days of madness while she was here—TV cameras, writers, photographers, and forty thousand people waiting in line to see her. And I was round the clock staying awake. She'd smash her head on the tank, get dizzy, and fall to the bottom. I'd jump in the tank and bring her up and get her going again and get out of the water real quickly. She'd go round for a while and then smash her head again. Finally, we said, 'Let's do something different. Let's turn her loose.' We took her to the Farallon Islands. Next time we'll know what to do. She taught us a lot.

"Last week we opened up our tropical penguin exhibit. Everybody thinks penguins are big tall birds sitting on an ice cube smoking Kools. There are seventeen different kinds of penguins, and almost all of them would freeze to death if you took them anywhere near the ice. They're flightless birds. I read everything ever known about penguins and discovered that the average bird is actually sitting in water about San Francisco's temperature, taking a shot at a subtropical fish swimming by. The puffins and murres that we all know from our own backyard are actually filling the same niche in the northern hemisphere; they're on their way to becoming penguins but they haven't quite made it.

"I'm also very interested in having scientists and researchers come in and take advantage of our facilities. I've given an open invitation to universities, fisheries people, anyone with a research project. Even people from PG & E came over, because they were interested in studying the sharks' sensitivity to electric fields.

"But the most important function of this aquarium will always be the education and delight for people who want to see the underwater world. We're lucky to be located in Golden Gate Park. Our overhead is very low, and we can afford to have children come in for only seventy-five cents. Every year we give thirty thousand tours led by docents. Membership for a year for a family is only twenty-five dollars and includes all kinds of activities. Then, there's a five-dollar summer membership, which includes classes and field trips in addition to as many visits to the aquarium as a kid could want. I feel like the luckiest guy in the world to be in charge of all this."

Chapter 44

Marine Education

California has 1,845 miles of coastline, and 80 percent of our population lives in coastal counties. This has long been the thrust of the argument of those trying to legitimize marine education in the public schools or to obtain funding for marine education in the private sector. Nobody was impressed. Most students graduated from high school knowing that the ocean west of California was named the Pacific by Balboa and that's it.

In 1976, a major change occurred: the area outward to two hundred miles at sea was incorporated into U.S. territory. Suddenly voters were being asked to decide on major issues of marine policy, whether it be fisheries, shipping, harbors, aquaculture, oil

leases, mineral leases, coastal development—a plethora of forma-
tive issues that will determine the shape of ocean policy for decades to come. The school system did not respond, however, and
marine education remained a stepchild. Today there's an impressive percentage of the voting public who don't know that California has a major commercial fishery, who don't know that the
tide goes in and out twice a day, who don't know the names of
even a few animals that swim along the beaches. It's an unhealthy
situation, when you consider that we, as a society, are looking to
the sea for salvation. One problem, of course, is lack of funds,
due to California's Proposition 13 which reduced property taxes,
and another is the recent lack of interest in the science curriculum
altogether. In 1984, California only had the equivalent of forty-
five full-time teachers of marine science.

The science curriculum in California is developed by a committee of thirty science educators who meet once every eight years
to write the framework. (Two years after that textbooks are
adopted; two years after that the curriculum is instituted; and
two years later it is again time to rewrite the framework.) Nineteen
eighty three was a framework year, and the earth science teachers
were adamant that the marine science program be expanded, to
no avail. Unfortunately, it appears that ocean science will remain,
at best, an elective course, offered in very few schools.

Practical considerations of a functioning democracy aside, can
you think of many things more likely to engage the mind of a child
than the mysteries of the sea? If you agree, and you don't want to
wait eight years for the next committee meeting, you can take
advantage of a remarkable number of programs that have sprung
up in the vacuum. Aquariums, museums, marine worlds, and
nonprofit organizations throughout the state, which have long
lobbied for ocean education, have within the last decade taken
large portions of their own monies to do the job themselves. Many
of these programs are free to the public, or available at nominal
fees.

Typical of these is Project Discovery, begun only five years
ago at Marineland in Palos Verdes. Every year fifty thousand kids
go through their programs—a lecture series on pinnipeds, ceta-
ceans, invertebrates, fishes, and the training of marine mammals,

with materials developed and adjusted for each age group; special education days for impaired kids; or the morning-long video and "meet the killer whales" session. Then there's the animal care rehabilitation program, where kids can learn about and participate in marine animal medicine, and the accredited teacher in-services, and the new outreach program, in which staff members are sent into the schools, often accompanied by a young sea lion who roams around the classroom luring the kids. Says Brad Andrews, curator of fishes and mammals at Marineland, "I sure never thought I'd be running a department of education!"

Typical also is the marine summer program given at Scripps Aquarium, with ten-session classes like Oscar Oceanographer for first to third graders or Marine Invertebrate Zoology for seventh to ninth graders, or the group field trips, which supply materials in Spanish and Spanish-speaking docents if requested. The list of organizations with strong marine education programs at the end of the book is only partial.

Despite the tremendous numbers being reached by these programs, they do have some drawbacks. For one thing, they depend on voluntary attendance, so naturally there is an inclination to attract people with entertainment—to bring out the popular starfish, sea anenomes, and sea lions; this is fine, but concepts are often ignored.

Something else ignored by these programs is the adult population. Most places don't bother with adults; others, like Scripps Aquarium, have tried and nobody comes. A few exceptions are the Oceanic Society in San Francisco, Palos Verdes Oceanographic Society, and the Cabrillo Museum in San Pedro. There is one entertainment/education program for adults, however, which has emerged in the last few years and has become wildly successful. Everybody gets up at five o'clock in the morning, meets down at the boat, and goes to sea looking for whales and birds or touring around the islands. Usually a naturalist goes along to answer questions, and it's a lyrical day away. These ocean trips are so popular that commercial party boats that used to hire out solely for fishing have seen the light. Places like H & M Landing in San Diego, one of the earliest to develop ocean nature expeditions, now has trips that combine skindiving, hiking on the southern islands, and shopping in Mexico, and trips that reach down as far as the Sea of Cortes and last up to ten days, with good food and all the trimmings. As you've no doubt guessed, these excursions aren't free. But if you look around, pick your season, and pull together your own group, chances are you can find an affordable trip from any port on the coast.

Naturally there are some aspects of marine knowledge that are not addressed in any of these programs. If you need to know about seafood handling, boating safety, building piers, ocean policy, wave erosion, finding fish, the economics of ocean industries, any one of a million things you might come across as the ocean plays a bigger and bigger role in our lives, you could flounder around a long time tracking down a source. But there *are* sources. Most folks are unaware that there are eleven people working for the state of California, with no other charge than to answer whatever marine-related question you may have—recreational, business, technological, abstract, or ridiculous. And if they can't answer you off the top of their head, then it's their job to find out.

In 1976, Congress passed the National Sea Grant College and Program Act, a recognizable adoption of the concepts of Land Grant passed one hundred years before. The byword of Sea Grant is "practical": practical research, practical techniques, and practical communication to all ocean users. The Marine Advisory program is the communication end of Sea Grant. (See the Marine Directory at the end of the book for the name, number, and address of your area advisor.) Each member of the team is assigned a county—in fact, most frequently he or she is selected from that community—and is expected to stay on top of all marine research being done at the university level, to become personally familiar with all marine industry and activities in the county, and then to be available to advise. Naturally, this is impossible. Most marine advisors develop expertise in a field that is relevant to their area and stay informed enough on other issues to have sources at their fingertips.

Another branch of Sea Grant annually puts out scores of pamphlets summarizing and simplifying the latest marine information, as you can see from the order form printed here. Sea Grant funds are also behind many of the kids' education programs throughout the state. All of this is free, and if you feel guilty about getting something for nothing, just remember the taxes you paid last April 15.

CALIFORNIA SEA GRANT

If you would like to receive CALIFORNIA SEA GRANT COLLEGE PROGRAM publications and announcements, please take a moment to fill out and return this card.

NAME _____ AFFILIATION _____

ADDRESS _____

CITY _____ STATE _____ ZIP CODE _____

☐ Coastal Zone Management (125) ☐ Aquaculture (107) ☐ Transportation (150)

☐ Coastal Geology & Hazards (166) ☐ Fisheries Enhancement (133) ☐ Recreation (144)

☐ Coastal Wetlands (153) ☐ Fisheries Product Development (163) ☐ Education (128)

☐ Ecology (145) ☐ Non-Living Resources (121) ☐ Chemistry/Toxicology (170)

☐ Marine Plants (167) ☐ Ocean Technology/Engineering (169) ☐ Marine Legislation (160)

☐ Marine Birds & Mammals (168) ☐ Ports & Harbors (149) ☐ Marine Economics (135)

Mail requests for California Sea Grant publications to: California Sea Grant College Program, University of California, A–032, La Jolla, CA 92093.

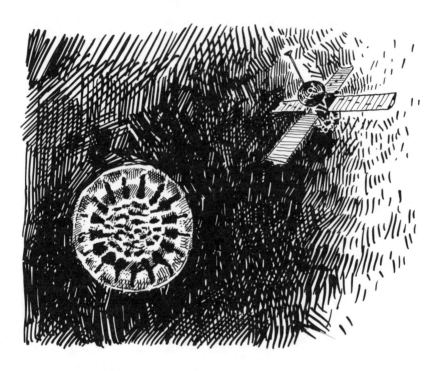

Chapter 45

Scripps Institute et al

Scripps Institute was founded in 1906 by a man named Joseph Ritter. Ritter was a scientist who used to pitch his tent at various outposts along the coast in a nomadic approach to studying the organisms of the tide pools and nearshore ecology. It was also in these tented halls of learning that he taught the students who were willing to come and wade in the sea.

Today, Scripps is eighty years old. It is the nation's oldest and largest oceanographic research center and the graduate school for the University of California and San Diego State University. Scripps employs eleven hundred people, and at any one time there are over two hundred fifty research projects under way, consuming an annual budget of $68 million a year. It's obviously impossible in this brief space to give even a cursory overview of its multitude of projects, as diverse as the many facets of the sea. But one thing that can be said with certainty after even the most casual glance is that the process of research today bears almost no resemblance to its roots of eighty years ago.

For example, take NORPAC, a project designed to determine the effect of the ocean on U.S. weather, particularly the fluctuations in our winters. A joint project that was funded with millions and millions of dollars by the National Science Foundation and the Office of Naval Research, it drew on scientists and facilities from around the Pacific rim — from New Caledonia, South America, Australia, Japan. NORPAC was run by many layers of committees and topped by a massive bureaucratic organization. Or take DSDP, the Deep Sea Drilling Project, another consortium project composed of scientists from many universities around the world, but primarily from Scripps, joining together with Global Marine, itself a consortium of mine owners. In 1964, they set out on a worldwide geology expedition to study the crust of the earth by looking at the long sediment cores obtained by drilling thousands of holes into the crust of the earth, holes that in some places penetrated over a mile into the earth. The data gathering of both these projects is complete, and now satellite oceanography is the going thing — utilizing various parts of the electromagnetic spectrum to bounce off or pick up information from the ocean surface, which, it is hoped, can be correlated with everything from wind shear to cracks in the ice to concentrations of chlorophyll. Today's research involves great coordinated efforts among the military, industry, and academia. No doubt the computer is very much a part of this vast transformation. Says Robert Stevenson, a physical oceanographer, "The costs of going to sea are upwards of fifteen thousand dollars a day, and that's one thing that makes computer modeling attractive to all funding agencies — it's cheaper and more efficient."

Scripps Institute doesn't have a cigarette machine anywhere along its miles of hallways. So when I smelled the telltale aroma wafting from one of the labs, I walked right in to bum a cigarette. The whole room was lined, shelved, stacked, and wall-to-walled with computers, and the researcher was nose-to in a sea of print-outs. "And what are you studying?" I asked, after he generously handed me a pack.

"Anchovies," he said. "I'm studying the anchovy."

And I couldn't help but wonder if he would know the anchovy from the sardine if I placed the two in front of him. And I wondered if the higher the power of the telescope, the less you see of the whole picture. And I couldn't help thinking about the story of the blind men and the elephant. And I wondered if science by committee means that the one person with an idea that makes a quantum leap would be overruled by the majority. These are questions that in one form or another have been asked of all modern sciences, but they seem especially appropriate to the ocean, which was almost entirely neglected by the traditional approach of science.

Robert Stevenson is both a researcher in physical oceanography at Scripps and the liaison person to one of the campus's major funders. He, like many other scientists, is concerned about these very issues. "If you're under thirty and if you studied anything about the ocean at all in high school, you probably learned about plate tectonics as a fact. But the big research after World War II was to find Precambrian rocks on the seafloor, which everyone figured existed because the oceans were clearly ancient. God knows how many billions were spent all through the 1950s and early sixties trying to find these old parts of the ocean. But not one piece came back that was older than Cretaceous. And the people just said, 'Well, we're simply looking in the wrong place.' In the meantime there was a small group of guys looking at magnetic anomaly data, and everyone said, 'Well, that doesn't mean anything.' It finally took a couple of young mavericks who had the know-how to put the data together and the character to stand up to the group to say, 'What it means is that the whole seafloor is moving,' and they damn near got stoned out of town for that. It's always been tough for the maverick, but now there's no room for them at all in the big group projects that are organized with all kinds of damn committees."

Mia Tegner is experiencing the problem from a little different angle. She recently got her Ph.D. in marine biology and is one of the younger members of the research staff at Scripps. "I spent two years trying to get funding through NSF for a project to determine the effect of currents on larval distribution in kelp beds and just couldn't get it through. The proposals that get funded already have the data that show it's going to work. The easiest way to get funding is to do the research first.

"The system does not encourage innovation. It does not permit asking a question for which the answer is not already known. It's very difficult to start out in new directions. Of course, it affects how I think, and everyone else who is not a superstar in the business. I think about problems in terms of what can get funded."

I certainly didn't take anything approaching a census on the subject. I talked with only twenty or so researchers while I was there, and all of them felt there was no more stimulating environment with more cross-fertilization of ideas than could be found at Scripps. At the same time, many expressed concerns similar to those above about the way in which directions in research are being determined. And it made me think back to something that happened to me after I left my own graduate studies in the sciences.

When I first started fishing, I would hear the other fishermen talking about the wind "having all the earmarks of a blow," or "these fish sure look like they're getting ready to travel," or "bad water is moving into the area," and I'd wonder just exactly how they knew. So I would ask them, beg them, for an answer. But all I ever got was a shrug of the shoulders or a curt "Experience," which made me think they were completely unaware of what they were doing—until a small incident occurred that caused me to rethink a whole lot of things.

There used to be a law in California that at a certain time of the year you could catch a king salmon, but not a silver. It was yet another dysfunctional law because once you hooked a fish with the kinds of hooks we were using back then, the chances were pretty good that the fish was going to die, especially a silver because their mouths are tender and rip easily, and the fish would likely bleed to death. But that's not my point. One day I had come in to unload and was boarded by the Fish and Game people. They wanted to check my catch for silvers. This was no problem to me, because there was a long unloading line and I had some cleaning up to do in the forecastle. "Go ahead," I said. "Take your time." So I cleaned up a little and looked back to the stern where the warden was still checking the fish. And I cleaned some more, until pretty soon the boat was cleaner than I can stand it. So I walked to the back deck and saw that he was doing something with the tails, and I said, "For Christ's sake, what are you doing with the fish?" And he answered me smartly, "What's the matter? Don't you know how to tell the difference between a king and a silver? You count the ridges on the tails—a king has this many ridges and a silver has that many ridges." I won't repeat what was said next, other than to say the conversation went rapidly downhill. Because I can guarantee that there isn't a fisherman on the coast who knows how many ridges are on the tail of this salmon or that. But if you hold up a fish clear on the other side of the dock, the fisherman can tell whether it's a king or a silver. In fact, he could tell what kind of fish it is before it even comes up out of the water just by its behavior or mood on the line—the kind of difference that could not be successfully conveyed to someone who has never experienced it.

But it made me think: this knowledge, about the ridges on the tail, was only a crutch for the lack of knowledge. This knowledge that we spend billions of dollars every year to collect from the ocean is framed in questions that are designed in such a way as to squeeze the essence and the spirit from the sea—all that makes us think, and feel, and care.

Marine Directory

The following directory is in no way meant to be comprehensive. It is merely a compilation of addresses and phone numbers that I came across in the course of working on this book and gleanings from the files of a few organizations like the Oceanic Society and the Pacific Coast Federation of Fishermen. The categorization is also, in places, quite arbitrary. For example, many of the groups listed under Marine Education could have been as appropriately placed under Research Organizations. My intention is only to provide you with a door to the ocean community, certain that you'll find your own way from there.

Aquaculture

Animal Science Department
University of California
Davis, CA 95616
(916) 752-1250

Aquaculture Advisory Committee
Chico Game Fish Farm
971 East Avenue
Chico, CA 95926
(916) 343-1849

Aquaculture Extension
University of California
Davis, CA 93123
(916) 752-7490

Aquaculture Magazine
P.O. Box 2329
Ashville, NC 28802

Aquatic Systems Incorporated
P.O. Box 8301
La Jolla, CA 92038
(619) 454-9005

California Aquaculture
Association
P.O. Box 1004
Niland, CA 92257
(619) 348-0547

Directory of California Aquaculture Association Members, Products, and Services
P.O. Box 1004
Niland, CA 92257
(619) 348-0457

Fish and Disease Laboratory
2111 Nimbus Road
Rancho Cordova, CA 95670
(916) 355-0811

Commercial Fisheries

California COFI Coordinator
University of California
La Jolla, CA 92093
(619) 453-2820

California Seafood Institute
1127 11th St., Suite 1003
Sacramento, CA 95814
(916) 447-4068

Department of Fisheries
Humboldt State University
Arcata, CA 95521
(707) 826-3954

InterAmerican Tropical Tuna
Association
8504 La Jolla Shores Drive
La Jolla, CA 92038
(619) 453-2820

Kelco
3355 Aero Drive
San Diego, CA 92123
(619) 292-4100

Pacific Coast Federation of
Fishermen's Associations, Inc.
3000 Bridgeway Building
Sausalito, CA 94966
(415) 332-5080

Pacific Coast Fishermen's Wives
Association
St. Rt. So. P.O. Box 3042
South Beach, OR 97366

Pacific Seafood Processors
Association
1620 South Jackson St.
Seattle, WA 98144
(206) 328-1205

Sea Grant MAP Extension
University of California
Davis, CA 95616
(916) 752-1497

Southwest Fisheries Center
P.O. Box 271
La Jolla, CA 92038
(619) 453-2820

U.S. Tuna Foundation
2040 Harbor Island Drive #208
San Diego, CA 92101
(619) 298-4697

West Coast Fisheries Development
Foundation
812 S.W. Washington Street,
Suite 900
Portland, OR 97025
(503) 222-3518

Western Fishboat Owners
Association
5055 N. Harbor Drive, Suite A
San Diego, CA 92106
(619) 224-2475

Federal Government Offices

Capital Information Switchboard
(202) 224-3121

Channel Islands National Park
1901 Spinnaker Drive
Ventura, CA 93001
(805) 644-8262

Coastal Zone Management,
Office of
National Oceanic and Atmospheric
Administration
1300 Whitehaven Street NW
Washington, DC 20235
(202) 347-6643

Environmental Protection Agency
215 Fremont St.
San Francisco, CA 94105
(415) 974-8017

Fleet Numerical Weather Facility
Presidio
Monterey, CA 93943
(408) 646-2141

Mineral Management Service
1340 West Sixth Street, Suite 244
Los Angeles, CA 90017
(213) 688-6990

National Academy of Sciences
2101 Constitution Avenue NW
Washington, DC
Marine Board (202) 389-6602
Ocean Science Board (202)
    389-6986
Naval Studies (202) 389-6755
Ocean Policy Committee (202)
    389-6813

National Marine Fisheries Service
Regional Director
300 S. Ferry Street
Terminal Island, CA 90731
(213) 548-2575

National Oceanic and Atmospheric
Administration (NOAA)
Department of Commerce
Washington, DC 20230
(202) 655-4000

National Weather Service
San Francisco (415) 876-2886
Los Angeles (213) 209-7211
San Diego (619) 297-2107

Pacific Fisheries Management
Council
526 SW Mill Street
Portland, OR 97201
(503) 221-6352

Point Reyes–Farallon Islands
National Park
Point Reyes, CA 94956
(415) 663-8522

Tijuana Sanctuary
3990 Old Town Avenue,
Suite 300 C
San Diego, CA 92110
(619) 237-6768

U.S. Army Corps of Engineers
P.O. Box 2711
Los Angeles, CA 90053
(213) 688-5522

U.S. Coast Guard (Twelfth
District)
Government Island
Alameda, CA 94501
(415) 437-3171

U.S. Coast Guard (Eleventh
District)
400 Oceangate
Long Beach, CA 90822
(213) 590-2305

U.S. Fish and Wildlife Service
Regional Director
500 Multnomah Street, Suite 1692
Portland, OR 97732

U.S. Fish and Wildlife Service
5758 West Century
Los Angeles, CA 90045
(213) 215-2033

Magazines

*Current: The Journal of Marine
Education*
P.O. Box 666
Narragansett, RI 02882
(302) 738-2324

Fishermen's News
C3 Building, Room 110
Fishermen's Terminal
Seattle, WA 98119
(206) 282-7545

Friday
Pacific Coast Federation of
Fishermen
3000 Bridgeway Building
Sausalito, CA 94966
(415) 332-5080

Greenpeace Examiner
2007 K Street NW
Washington, DC 20009
(202) 462-1177

Latitude 38
P.O. Box 1678
Sausalito, CA 94966
(415) 383-8200

Maritime Humanities Newsletter
Fort Mason Foundation
Laguna and Marina Boulevard
San Francisco, CA 94123
(415) 673-0797

National Fishermen
4215 21st Avenue West
Seattle, WA 98199
(206) 283-1150

Oceans Magazine
Fort Mason Center
San Francisco, CA 94123
(415) 441-1104

Oceanus
Woods Hole Oceanographic
Institute
Woods Hole, MA 02543
(617) 548-1400

Pacific Fishing
1515 NW 51st Street
Seattle, WA 98107
(206) 789-5333

San Diego Log
1017 Rosecrans
San Diego, CA 92106
(619) 226-1608

Sea Frontiers
International Oceanographic
Foundation
3919 Rickenbacker Causeway
Virginia Key, Miami, FL 33149
(305) 361-5786

Sea Pacific Skipper
419 Old Newport Boulevard
Newport Beach, CA 12663
(714) 645-1611

Sea Technology
1117 North 19th Street
Arlington, VA 22209
(703) 524-3136

Wooden Boat Magazine
P.O. Box 78
Brookline, ME 04616
(207) 359-4651

Marine Advisors

California's Sea Grant Marine Advisors

Del Norte & Curry Counties
James Waldvogel
Del Norte County
Courthouse Annex
981 H Street
Crescent City, CA 95531
(707) 464-4711

Humboldt County
Christopher Toole
Marine Advisory Service
Foot of Commercial Street
Eureka, CA 95501
(707) 443-8369

Marin, Sonoma, & Mendocino Counties
Bruce Wyatt
2604 Ventura Avenue, Room 100-P
Santa Rosa, CA 95401
(707) 527-2621

San Francisco Bay Counties
Connie Ryan
Marine Advisory Service
P.O. Box 34066
San Francisco, CA 94134
(415) 586-4115

Monterey & Santa Cruz Counties
Edward Melvin
1432 Freedom Boulevard
Watsonville, CA 95076
(408) 724-4734

San Luis Obispo, Santa Barbara, Ventura, Los Angeles, & Orange Counties
John Richards
377 Storke Road
Goleta, CA 93117-2949
(805) 968-2149

San Diego County
Art Flechsig
5555 Overland Drive, Bldg. 4
San Diego, CA 92123
(619) 565-5572

Marine Advisory Specialists

Aquaculture
Fred S. Conte

Aquaculture Extension
University of California
Davis, CA 95616
(916) 752-7490

Marine Fisheries
Chris Dewees
Sea Grant MAP Extension
University of California
Davis, CA 95616
(916) 752-1497

Seafood Technology
Robert J. Price*
Food Science and Technology
University of California
Davis, CA 95616
(916) 752-2191

Marine Education

Cabrillo Museum
3720 Stephenwhite Drive
San Pedro, CA 90831
(213) 548-7562

California Marine Mammal Center
Golden Gate National Recreation Area
Sausalito, CA 94965
(415) 331-0161

California Maritime Academy
P.O. Box 1392
Vallejo, CA 02453
(707) 644-5601

*The Marine Advisory Program is co-ordinated by Robert J. Price at the program's main office in the Department of Food Science and Technology, University of California, Davis, CA 95616, (916) 752-2191

Center for Environmental
Education
624 9th Street NW
Washington, DC 20001
(202) 737-3600

Coordinator of Marine Advisors
Sea Grant and MAP Extension
University of California
Davis, CA 95616
(916) 752-2193

Directory of Academic Marine
Programs in California
Institute of Marine Resources
University of California
La Jolla, CA 92093
(619) 452-2230

Manager of Science Education
State Board of Education
721 Capitol Mall
Sacramento, CA 95814
(916) 324-7187

Marine Land Education
Department
6610 Palos Verdes Drive South
Rancho Palos Verdes, CA 90274
(213) 541-5663

Monterey Bay Aquarium
886 Cannery Row
Monterey, CA 93940
(408) 649-6466

National Marine Education
Association
P.O. Box 666
Narragansett, RI 02882
(401) 789-8022

Oceanic Society
Building E
Fort Mason Center
San Francisco, CA 94123
(415) 441-1104

Point Reyes Bird Observatory
Shoreline Highway
Stinson Beach, CA 94970
(415) 868-1221

San Francisco Bay Model
2100 Bridgeway
Sausalito, CA 94965
(415) 332-3870

Scripps Aquarium
La Jolla Shores Drive
La Jolla, CA 92093
(619) 452-4086

Sea World San Diego
1720 South Shores Road
San Diego, CA 92109
(619) 224-3562

Steinhart Aquarium
Golden Gate Park
San Francisco, CA 94118
(415) 221-5100

Union Oil Animal Care Center
6610 Palos Verdes Drive South
Rancho Palos Verdes, CA 90274
(213) 541-5663

The Whale Center
3929 Piedmont Avenue
Oakland, CA 94611
(415) 654-6621

Yosemite Institute
Golden Gate National Recreation
Area
Sausalito, CA 94965
(415) 332-5771

Nonprofit Groups

California Coastal Conservancy
1330 Broadway, Suite 1100
Oakland, CA 94612

California Sportfishing Alliance
P.O. Box 725
Dunsmuir, CA 96025

Environmental Defense Fund
2602 Dwight Way
Berkeley, CA 94704
(415) 548-8906

The Farallon Project
P.O. Box 9
Bolinas, CA 94924

Friends of the Earth
1045 Sansome Street
San Francisco, CA 94111

Friends of the River
1228 N Street, Room 24
Sacramento, CA 95814
(916) 442-3155

Friends of the Sea Otter
P.O. Box 220, 221
Carmel, CA 93922
(408) 625-3290

Greenpeace
Building G, Fort Mason Center
San Francisco, CA 94123
(415) 474-6767

International Bird Rescue
Aquatic Park
Berkeley, CA 94710
(415) 841-9086

National Wildlife Federation
1412 16th Street NW
Washington, DC 20036
(202) 797-6800

Natural Resources Defense Council
25 Kearny St.
San Francisco, CA 94108
(415) 421-6561

Salmon Unlimited
19231 Summers Lane
Fort Bragg, CA 92100

Sierra Club
1228 N Street
Sacramento, CA 95814
(916) 444-2180

Research

Bodega Bay Marine Labs
P.O. Box 247
Bodega Bay, CA 94923
(707) 875-2211

Center for Coastal Marine Studies
University of California
Santa Cruz, CA 95064
(408) 429-0111

Center for Marine Studies
San Diego State University
San Diego, CA 92182
(619) 265-5200

Hopkins Marine Station
Pacific Grove, CA 93950
(408) 373-0464

Hubbs Sea World Research
Institute
1700 South Shores Road
San Diego, CA 92109
(619) 224-3562

Institute for Marine and Coastal
Studies
University of Southern California
Los Angeles, CA 90007
(213) 743-6104

Marine Science Institute
University of California
Santa Barbara, CA 93106
(805) 961-2311

Moss Landing Marine Labs
P.O. Box 223
Moss Landing, CA 95039–0223
(408) 633-3304

National Marine Fisheries Service
Tiburon Station
3150 Paradise Drive
Tiburon, CA 94920
(415) 435-3149

Pacific Bio Marine Labs
P.O. Box 536
Venice, CA 90291
(213) 822-5757

Pacific Ocean Policy Studies
74 Roosevelt Circle
Palo Alto, CA 94306
(415) 497-2300

Scripps Institute
La Jolla, CA 92093
(619) 452-2230

Southern California Ocean Studies
Consortium
California State University
Long Beach, CA 90840
(213) 498-4111

Southwest Fisheries Center
P.O. Box 271
La Jolla, CA 92038
(619) 453-2820

State Mussel Watch
Department of Fish and Game
2201 Garden Road
Monterey, CA 93904
(408) 649-2870

Tiburon Center for Environmental
Studies
San Francisco State University
P.O. Box 855
Tiburon, CA 94920
(415) 435-1717

Sports and Recreation

Central California Council of
Divers
P.O. Box 779
Daly City, CA 94071
(415) 583-8492

Greater Los Angeles Council of
Divers
P.O. Box 1533
Beverly Hills, CA 90213
(805) 647-5141

Northern California Federation of
Fly Fishers
90 East Gish Road, Suite 3A
San Jose, CA 95112
(408) 292-2534

Professional Association of Diving
Instructors
1243 E. Warner Avenue
Santa Ana, CA 92705–0550

San Diego Council of Divers
P.O. Box 9259
San Diego, CA 92109
(619) 579-6307

Southwest Council
Federation of Fly Fishermen
621 Westover Place
Pasadena, CA 91105
(213) 799-5066

United Anglers
1316 Nielson Street
Berkeley, CA 94702
(415) 526-4049

United States Power Squadron
District 25 (Northern California)
280 Summit Avenue
San Rafael, CA 94901
(415) 454-8663

United States Power Squadron
District 13 (Southern California)
1976 Dunnigan Street
Camarillo, CA 93010

Valley Council of Divers
4844 Holyoke Way
Sacramento, CA 95841
(916) 344-3109

State Government Agencies

State Government Information
(916) 322-9900

California Coastal Commission
631 Howard Street
San Francisco, CA 94106
(415) 543-8555

California Coastal Commission
P.O. Box 1450
Long Beach, CA 90801
(213) 590-5071

Department of Boating and
Waterways
1629 S Street
Sacramento, CA 95814
(916) 445-2615

Environmental Policy Specialist
Senate Office of Research
1100 J Street, Suite 500
Sacramento, CA 95814
(916) 445-1721

Hazardous Waste Materials
1219 K Street
Sacramento, CA 95814
(916) 322-2337

Joint Committee on Fisheries and
Aquaculture
1127 11th Street, Suite 605
Sacramento, CA 95814
(916) 326-0324

San Francisco Bay Conservation
and Development Commission
30 Van Ness Avenue
San Francisco, CA 94102
(415) 557-3686

State Agency Coordinator Oil and
Hazardous Materials
Department of Fish and Game
1416 Ninth Street
Sacramento, CA 95814
(916) 445-3531

State Department of Fish and Game
1416 Ninth Street
Sacramento, CA 95814
(916) 445-3531

State Department of Fish and Game
245 W. Broadway, Suite 350
Long Beach, CA 90802
(213) 590-5132

State Department of Fish and Game
411 Burgess Drive
Menlo Park, CA 94025
(415) 326-0324

State Department of Fish and Game
619 2nd Street
Eureka, CA 95501
(707) 442-1402

State Department of Parks and
Recreation
1416 Ninth Street, 14th Floor
Sacramento, CA 95814
(916) 445-6744

State Lands Commission
1807 13th Street
Sacramento, CA 95814
(916) 322-4105

State Water Resources Control
Board
1416 Ninth Street
Sacramento, CA 95814
(916) 445-3157

Index